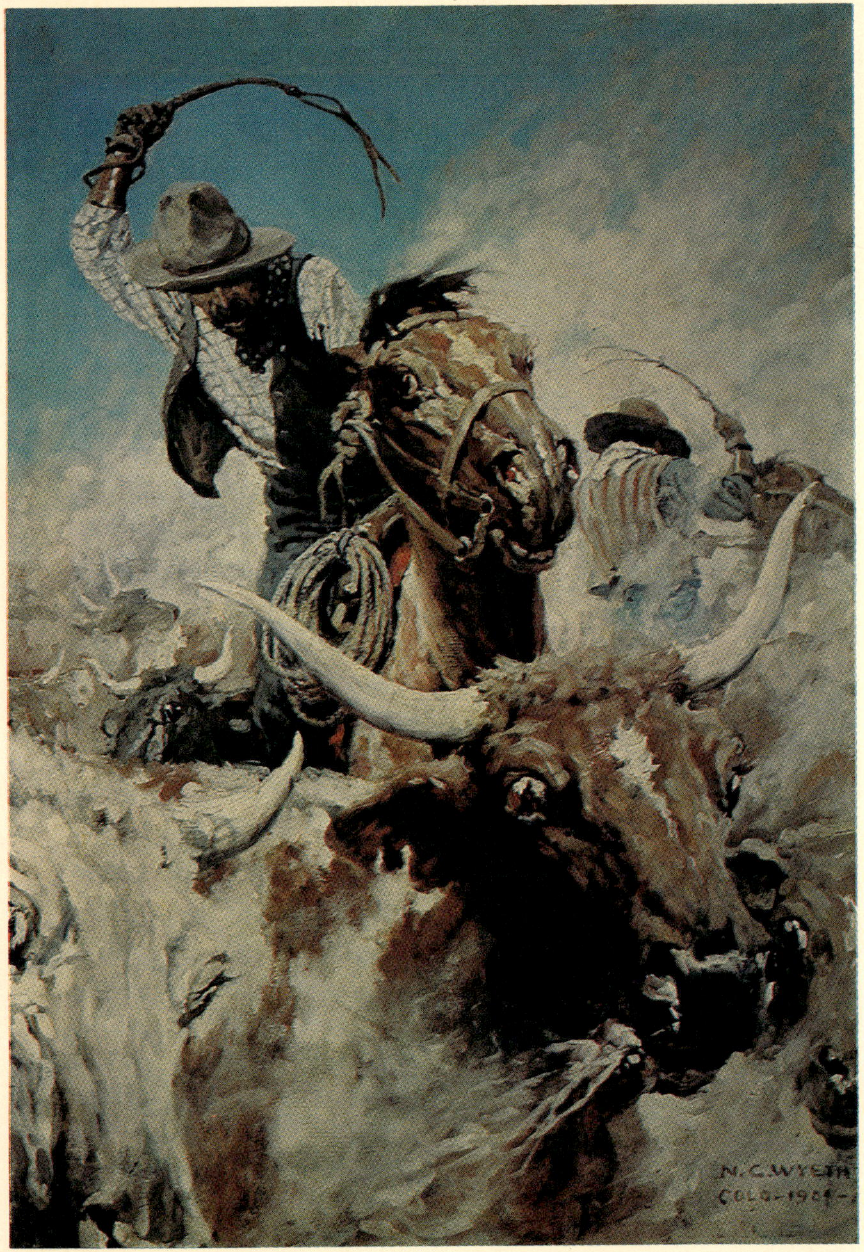

COWBOY

A Special Exhibition at the
Buffalo Bill Historical Center
Exhibition and Catalogue prepared by Don Hedgpeth

Distributed by University of Nebraska Press
901 North 17th Street; Lincoln, Nebraska 68588
ISBN 0–8032–6304–X

COWBOY   by Don Hedgpeth

The broad, wide-open country had once been the grazing grounds for vast herds of buffalo. By the 1870's the buffalo were about all gone, and so too were most of the warring Indians who had depended on them. Wyoming ranges were big, empty and peaceful; hundreds of miles of nothing but free grass, rushing water, lofty mountains and clean, clear air.

There were over a hundred varieties of native grass. Lush bluestem, gramma and buffalo grass cured on the ground in the dry climate and provided nutritious feed year round. In 1871, a four year old grass-fed steer, raised from a calf on the Laramie Plains, yielded 982 pounds of meat, with two inches of fat on his ribs.

Rivers with names like Chugwater, Tongue, Belle Fourche, Platte, Wind, Powder and countless creeks and streams provided a generous supply of fresh water for cow operations in every region of the state. Snowmelt gave a head start for spring grass growth each year. It was an ideal cow country, bountifully endowed with all the necessities for producing beef.

The trail driving era began in earnest in 1866 when one half million longhorns were trailed north from Texas to the shipping pens of the wild Kansas cow towns. The following year, the Union Pacific, moving westward across the Great Plains, reached Cheyenne. Wyoming, with over fifty million acres of unfenced grasslands was destined to be cow country.

Wyoming's first permanent beef herd was established by W. G. Bullock and B. B. Mills on the Laramie Plains in 1868. By the mid 1880's, the open range cattle industry was at its heighth. Rapid expansion, heavy foreign investment and the sheer magnitude of operations in Wyoming's cow country reflected all of the most glorious aspects of the rawhide times of free grass and self-reliant double tough cowboys. Early Wyoming developed and prospered in direct proportion to the growth and success of her cattle industry. The cow made Wyoming something of which the West will always be proud.

A sizeable portion of the early Wyoming cowboys were Texas men. They had followed the longhorns north to a country where abundant grass and water made a land that looked like it would be cow country forever. There were also Colorado hands who came in with the herds of John Iliff, the first man to trail cattle into the newly built pens at Cheyenne in 1867. The Wyoming range was home too for many boys from the British Isles who craved the adventure and rugged life of the cow camp.

They were all men of whang leather toughness. Some of them were like the horses they rode—"they would not do to monkey with." The harshness of their life was reflected in their creased, tanned faces and in the bow of their legs and the stoop of their shoulders.

Cowboys became as natural a part of outdoor Wyoming as the antelope and deer. A good cowboy lived in harmony, when he could, with nature. It was a life close to the ground. The men who chose it were "bound to be wild and brave." Wyoming cowboys were truly "men with guts and horses."

The long days of spring and fall roundups seemed never to end. It was riding circle, cutting and shaping cattle, castrating and branding, night herding and long dusty drives to the shipping points. By the time a roundup was over a cowboy "could sleep standing up like his horse."

Being a range cowboy anywhere was a tough chore. Weather added extra harshness in Wyoming's cow country. Riding the ranch boundaries and tailing up poor cattle in deep snow and bitter cold called for rugged men. And there were always men to take on the job; men who never failed to laugh at every hardship and danger.

After years of cowboying for meager wages they had nothing but the experience to show for it, and they generally had paid a good price for that. It was all hard work when there was work to be done. But there was dignity in doing it horseback. Half broke horses that could kick a chew of tobacco out of your mouth, and snorty mama cows kept it from being boring. They used to like to boast that they "could go anywhere a cow would and stand anything a horse could."

There was a large measure of independence to life on the Wyoming range. Self-reliance and vitality were essential qualities of a top hand. The men took pride in their kind of life and in the cow work they did. Loyalty to the brand they rode for was a strong bond between the men of a particular outfit. "They would follow their wagon boss through hell and never complain."

It was a life of early mornings, long days and short nights. Plain, hardy food and plenty of horseback work kept the fat trimmed from their frames. "They live on little and are as loyal in their promises and their sympathies as they are ardent in their vengeance." Life in a line shack during a Wyoming winter made a man more alone than any man ever was.

The Wyoming cowboy had a taste of genuine life, and while it lasted, he savored every bit of it. His motto was: "Take her as she comes and like it."

The cow country heritage is still strong in Wyoming. The foundations of the state were laid on hide and horn. There is still loyalty to the cow and the industry she produced.

In spite of killing winters, drought, depression, bureaucrats and "conservationists", the cowman has endured. He has steadfastly spurned government subsidies, and, in the face of constantly rising operational costs, has maintained the independence and integrity of his industry.

New calves still hit the ground every spring and men still pack ropes on their saddles and go about the business of putting beef on the dinner table of America. The cattle are of a different kind, and the ranches are smaller, but the nature of the business and the spirit of the men who are involved in it are much the same as they were when drovers first crossed the Platte at Ogallala and headed west into one of God's most perfect cattle ranges. We at the Buffalo Bill Historical Center are pleased to salute Wyoming's cowboy heritage with the special exhibition.

The special 1975 Exhibition at the Buffalo Bill Historical Center is dedicated to the cowboy and to his large measures of self-reliance and vitality.

Included in this exhibition are several photographs of Wyoming range life from the early 1930's. The man who captured these fleeting scenes of the cowboy's life was Charles Belden. The pictures were taken on the historic Pitchfork Ranch near Meeteetse, Wyoming, just to the south of Cody. The photographs preserve the look of the cow country as it was undergoing the transition from the free grass open range to the fenced pasture and hay stack. An extensive collection of Belden's work is included in the archives of the Buffalo Bill Historical Center.

Paintings and sculpture by twenty-five fine artists have been selected for the Cowboy Exhibition. The techniques and styles represented are varied, as are the regions and periods of history depicted. Taken together, this collection offers a complete, colorful and exciting look at the men called cowboy.

CHARLES M. RUSSELL (1864-1926) is best known of all the artists who have painted and sculpted the cowboy. A cowboy himself on the early Montana range, Russell brought to his art a personal intimacy with the subject matter, as well as the talent of a truly fine artist.

FREDERIC REMINGTON (1861-1909) rode with the cowboy on ranges from Mexico to Canada. He captured, in his paintings and sculpture, the essence of the cowboy for all time. Remington's sculpture of "The Bronco Buster" is one of the best known examples of fine art representing the cowboy.

MELVIN WARREN (contemporary) is one of the most distinguished of modern artists to paint the cowboy. Warren is a Texan and finds abundant evidence to refute the often repeated statement that there are no more cowboys. He is an accomplished painter and his talent does credit to the story of the cowboy.

N. C. WYETH (1882-1945) is one of the most familiar names in American art. The subject matter of his paintings ranged from scenes of Robin Hood and Treasure Island to the rough action of the Colorado cow camps of 1904. The six Wyeth paintings included here were painted from life by the young artist.

W. H. D. KOERNER (1878-1938) was, like Wyeth, known for his popular illustrative work. Koerner was particularly attracted to western subjects. His work appeared with many of the cornerstones of western literature. Koerner was at ease around cowboys and depicted them well in many of his finest works.

BURT PROCTOR (contemporary) began drawing horses as a child. He became a trained painter and was one of the few stylistic innovators among the artists who painted cowboys. Proctor's paintings have an artistic substance that makes his subject matter a secondary consideration. He added a new dimension to the cowboy in art.

JAMES BAMA (contemporary) is a painter with sound foundations in formal art training and in the discipline of commercial art and illustration. His fine paintings of present day cow people capture a time in the cow country that is undergoing constant and dramatic change.

ROBERT LOUGHEED (contemporary) has produced some of the most highly acclaimed paintings of the modern cowboy. A long time visitor to New Mexico's historic Bell Ranch, Lougheed has seen and shared the cowboy's life. The quality of his paintings is widely recognized and his attention to authenticity is complete.

FRANK TENNEY JOHNSON (1874-1939) traveled and painted cowboy life throughout the western range country. Many of his paintings are of men and places right around Cody. Johnson was a fine artist in the term's most sophisticated sense. It is fortunate that a man with such abundant talent was inspired by the cowboy.

JAMES E. REYNOLDS (contemporary) is represented by some of the most substantial paintings in this exhibition. Although he is true to the physical appearance of cowboy life, Reynolds is primarily concerned with the techniques that produce quality painting. His work is assured of a significant place in the body of art depicting the cowboy.

BILL OWEN (contemporary) is not only a good painter of cowboy life, he is a good hand on horse-back. He paints scenes that he has participated in and thereby brings a personal element to his work that lends an additional substance. The colors of Owen's paintings reflect the Arizona cow country he knows as home.

NED JACOB (contemporary) highlights the landscapes of the western range with its particular values of light and color. He includes cowboys and cattle in his paintings as features that are sympathetic to the land. Jacob travels extensively and has painted ranch country scenes from Colorado to Mexico.

MAYNARD DIXON (1875-1946) attended art school in his native California and then became an itinerant cowboy in the desert country of the Southwest. His affection for cowboy life remained strong long after he became a highly acclaimed artist. This affection is reflected in the many paintings he produced with the cowboy as his subject.

OLAF WIEGHORST (contemporary) is among the best known of the contemporary painters of the cowboy. His paintings of ranch scenes are from the hot, dusty Southwest. The men and horses of Wieghorst's art clearly show how much the old and the modern cow country have in common.

FRANK HOFFMAN (1888-1958) was one of the members of the distinguished Taos Society of Artists. He enjoyed success as a commercial artist and illustrator, as well as producing fine western paintings. Hoffman was influenced by the techniques of impressionism. His paintings of range life add a refreshing variety to the total of the cowboy in art.

BOB MEYERS (1919-1970) left a highly successful career in commercial art to settle on a ranch close to Cody in 1960. He painted scenes from personal observation and horseback experience in today's Wyoming cow country. Meyers' paintings of cowboys were produced with the added bonus of the spectacular mountain scenery of Wyoming's high cattle ranges.

W. R. LEIGH (1866-1955) is one of the truly respected names in the story of western art. His cowboy paintings are highlighted by the action and vitality that were so much a part of the early range life. Leigh's work is included in the collections of all the major western art museums.

TOM LEA (contemporary) has significantly enhanced the story of the man on horseback with his paintings. His contribution is singular in the treatment of the Hispanic origins of the range cattle industry. The eleven paintings included in this exhibition, aside from their obvious artistic quality, are a remarkable historical document of the development of the cattle industry in America.

SOLON BORGLUM (1868-1922) was the brother of Gutzon Borglum, the sculptor of the four faces on Mt. Rushmore. Solon Borglum enjoyed a distinguished career in his own right. He had been a working cowboy on the Utah range in his youth and always favored the bow-legged men as subject matter for his sculpture.

EDWARD FRAUGHTON (contemporary) seeks inspiration for his sculpture in the pages of western history. The two sculptures included in this exhibition are proof that he has studied well. Fraughton's talent as a sculptor is abundant and his cowboy pieces are fitting tributes to the men of the range.

HARRY JACKSON (contemporary) is a sculptor whose talent is large enough to tell, in bronze, the epic story of the cowboy. His "Stampede" and "Range Burial" are milestones in the cowboy art tradition.

JOE BEELER (contemporary) is a widely known name in contemporary art of the cowboy. Beeler is both painter and sculptor. He is represented in this exhibition with examples of his cowboys in bronze. He has first hand knowledge of the life he represents in his art. His work is essential to any collection of the cowboy in art.

GRANT SPEED (contemporary) is himself a ranch country product. He carries on the cowboy artist tradition begun by Russell. His bronzes are clear evidence of his knowledge of cow country subject matter. Speed's sculpture includes the whole spectrum of range life, from the wild action of a bronc, to the quiet, reflective moments of a cowboy who realizes his is a fast fading way of life.

BOB SCRIVER (contemporary) has produced many fine sculptures of the old time cowboy. He has also executed a remarkable series of the modern rodeo cowboy. Scriver is a native of the Montana range country and has spent his entire life around men who are more comfortable horseback than on foot. Scriver's heroic sculpture of Bill Linderman is one of the finest of all the artistic tributes to the cowboy.

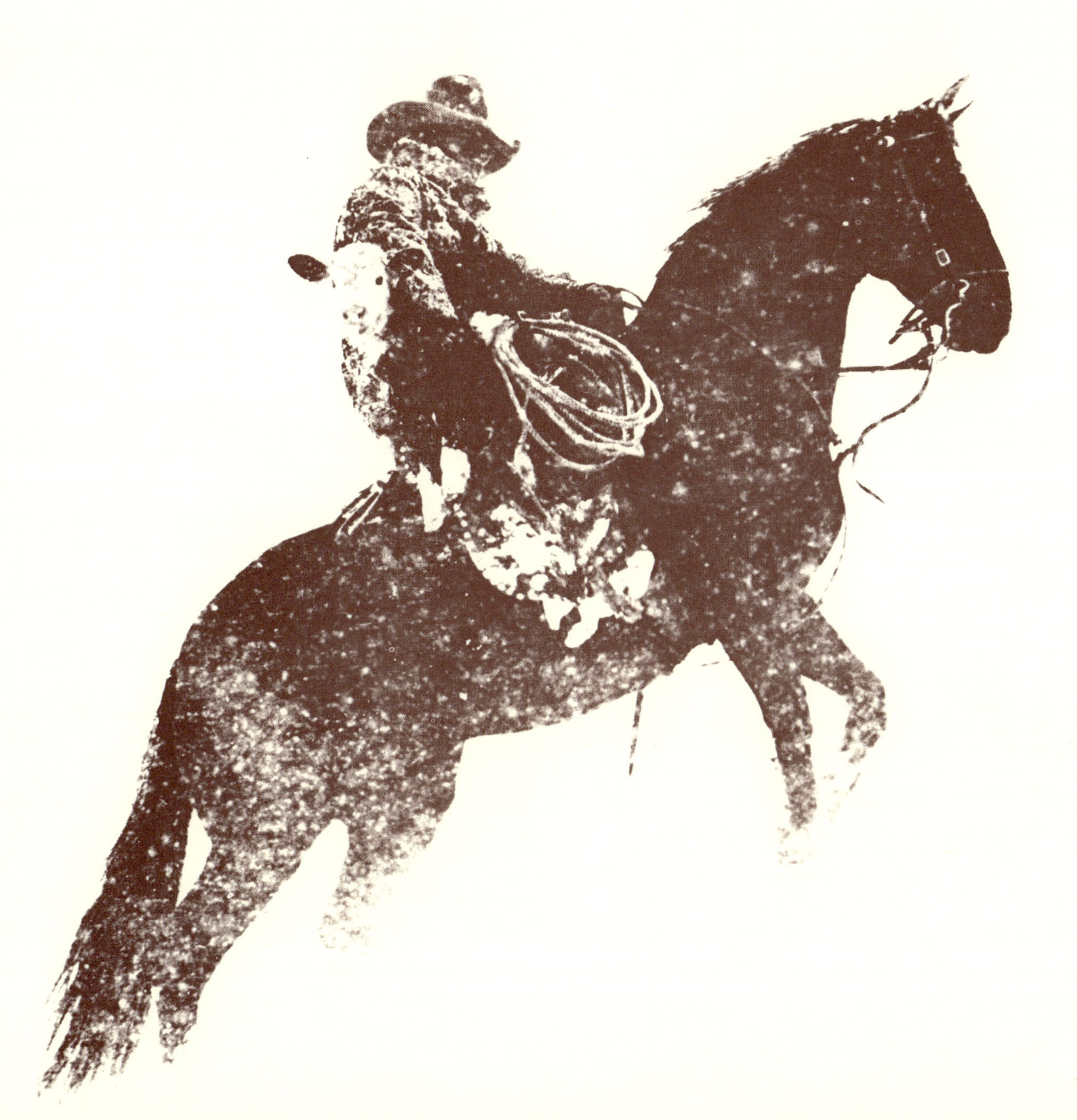

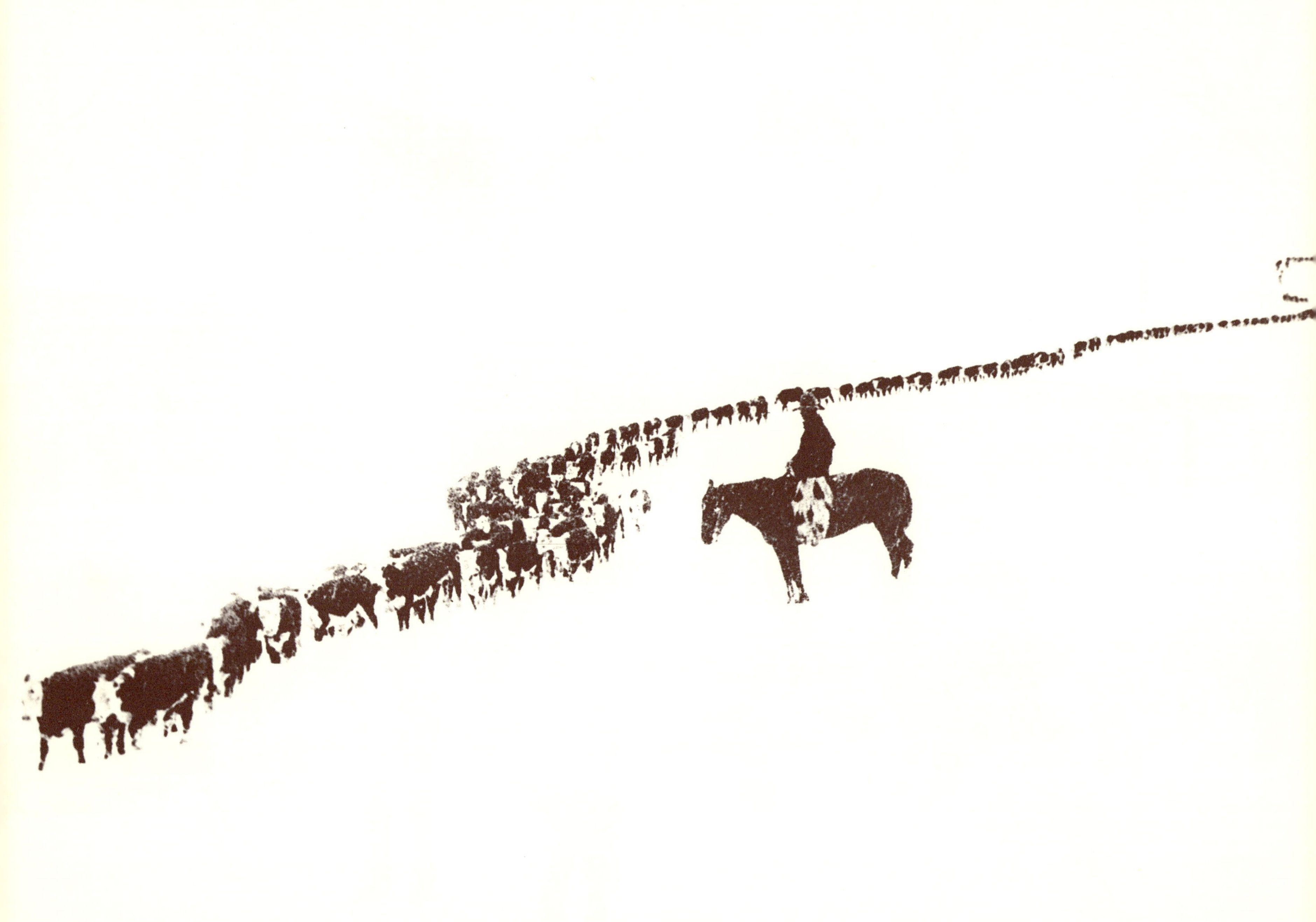

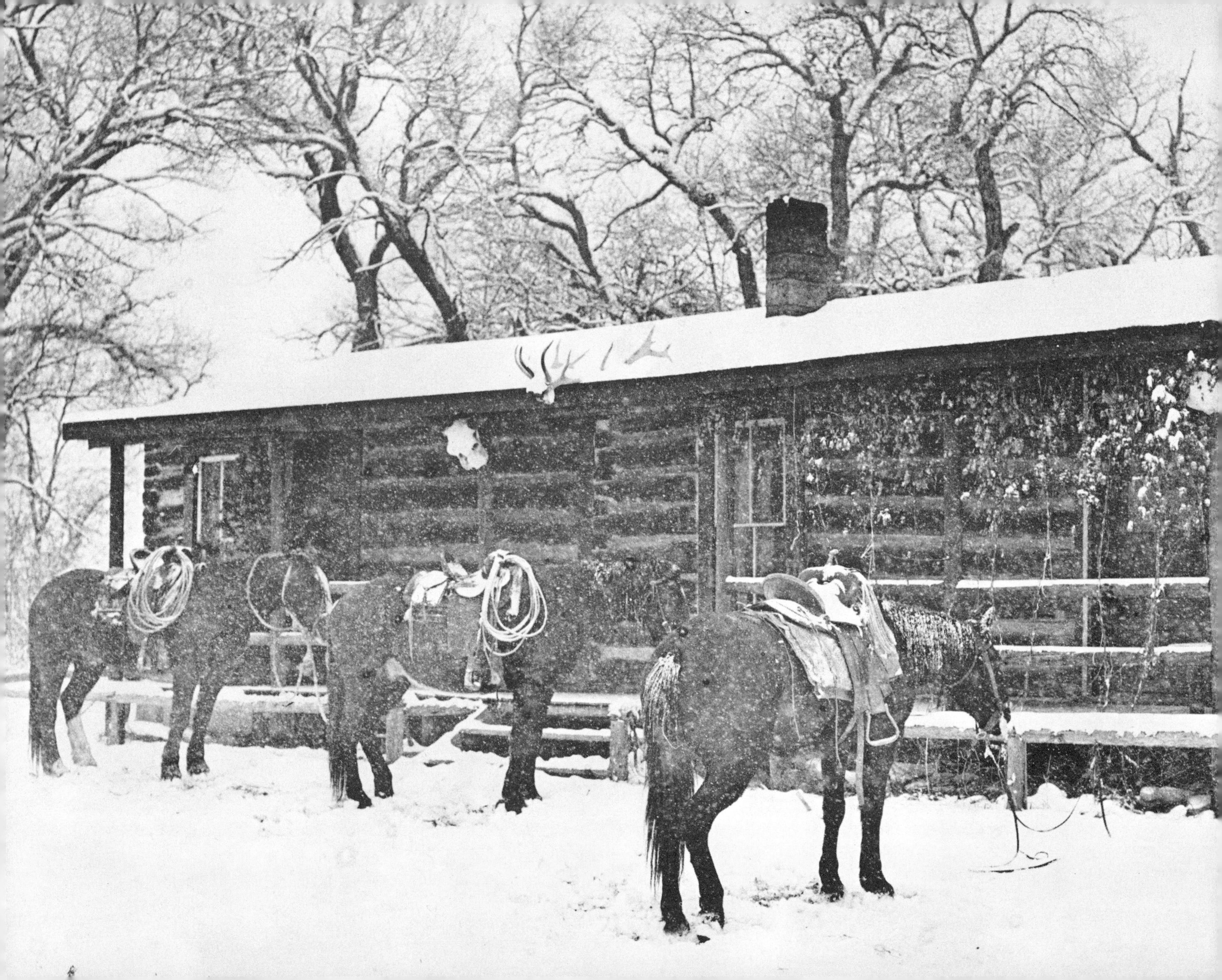

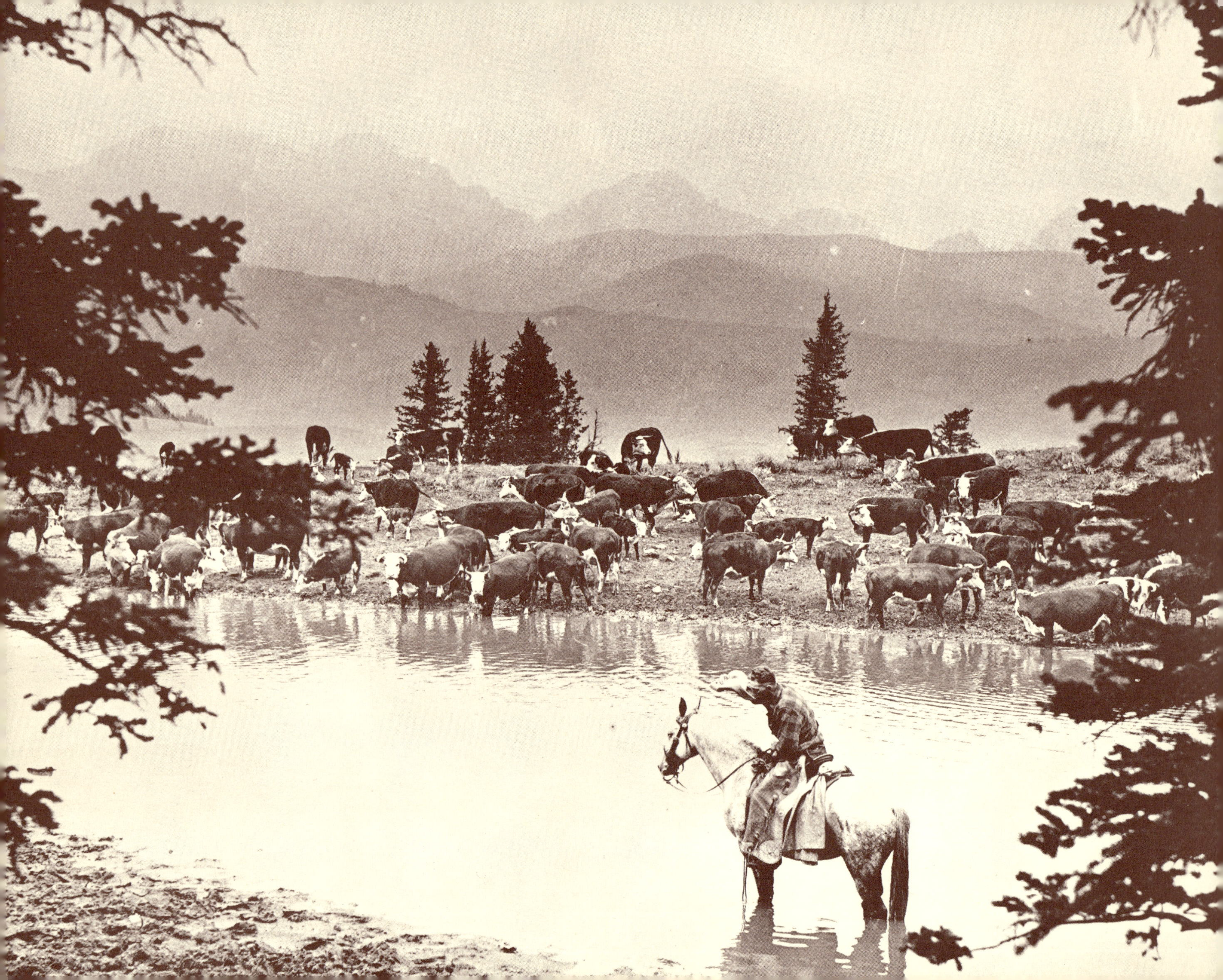

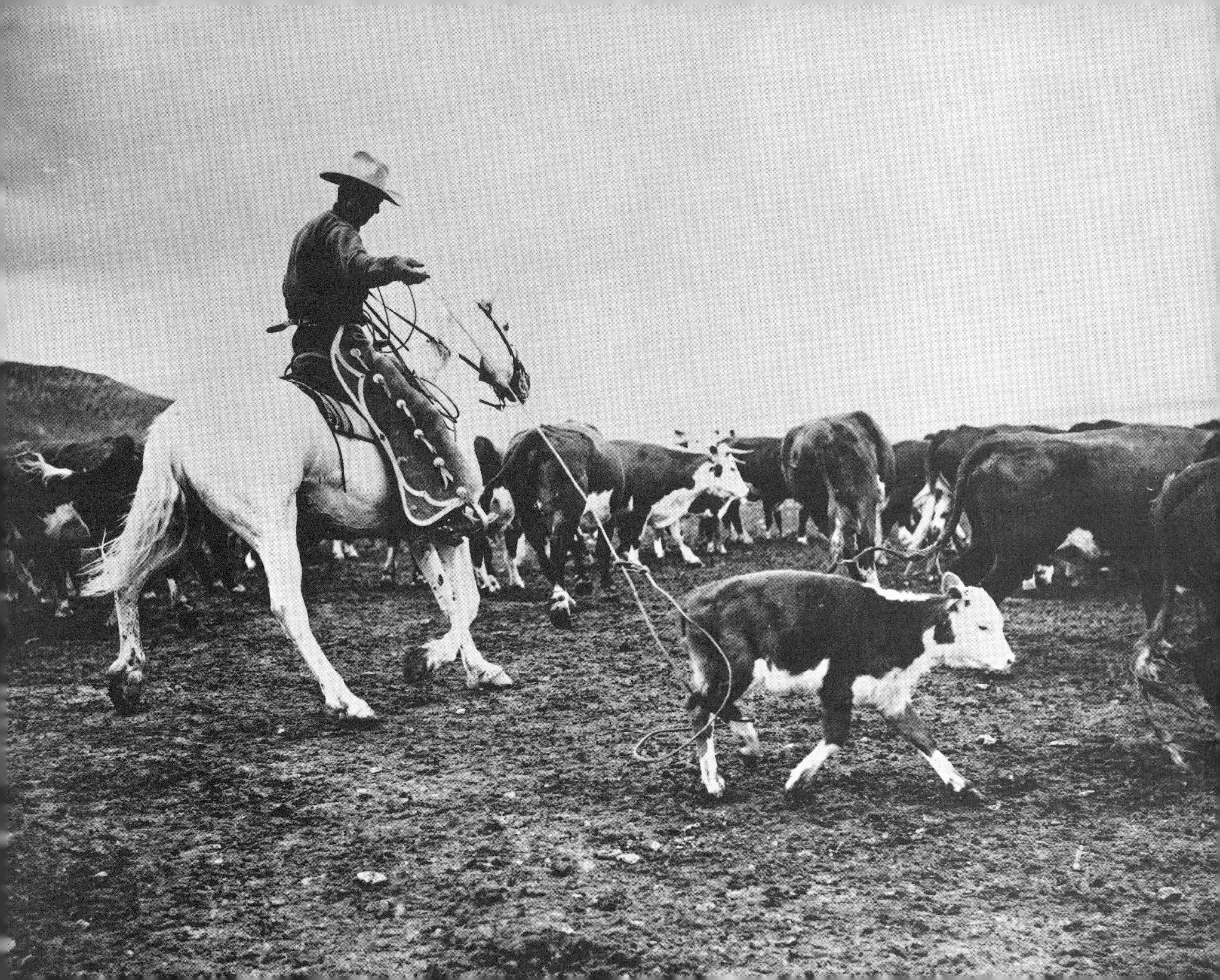

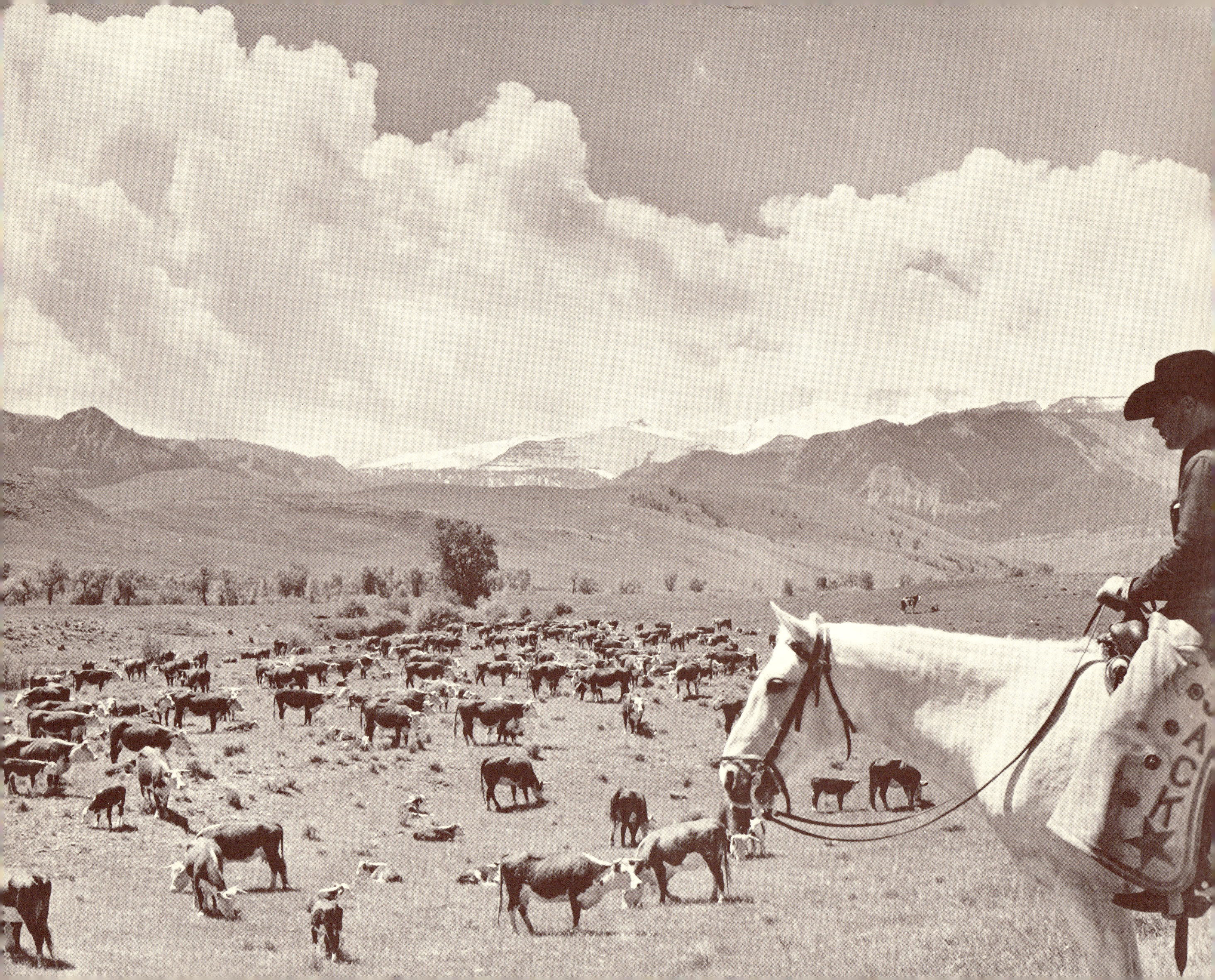

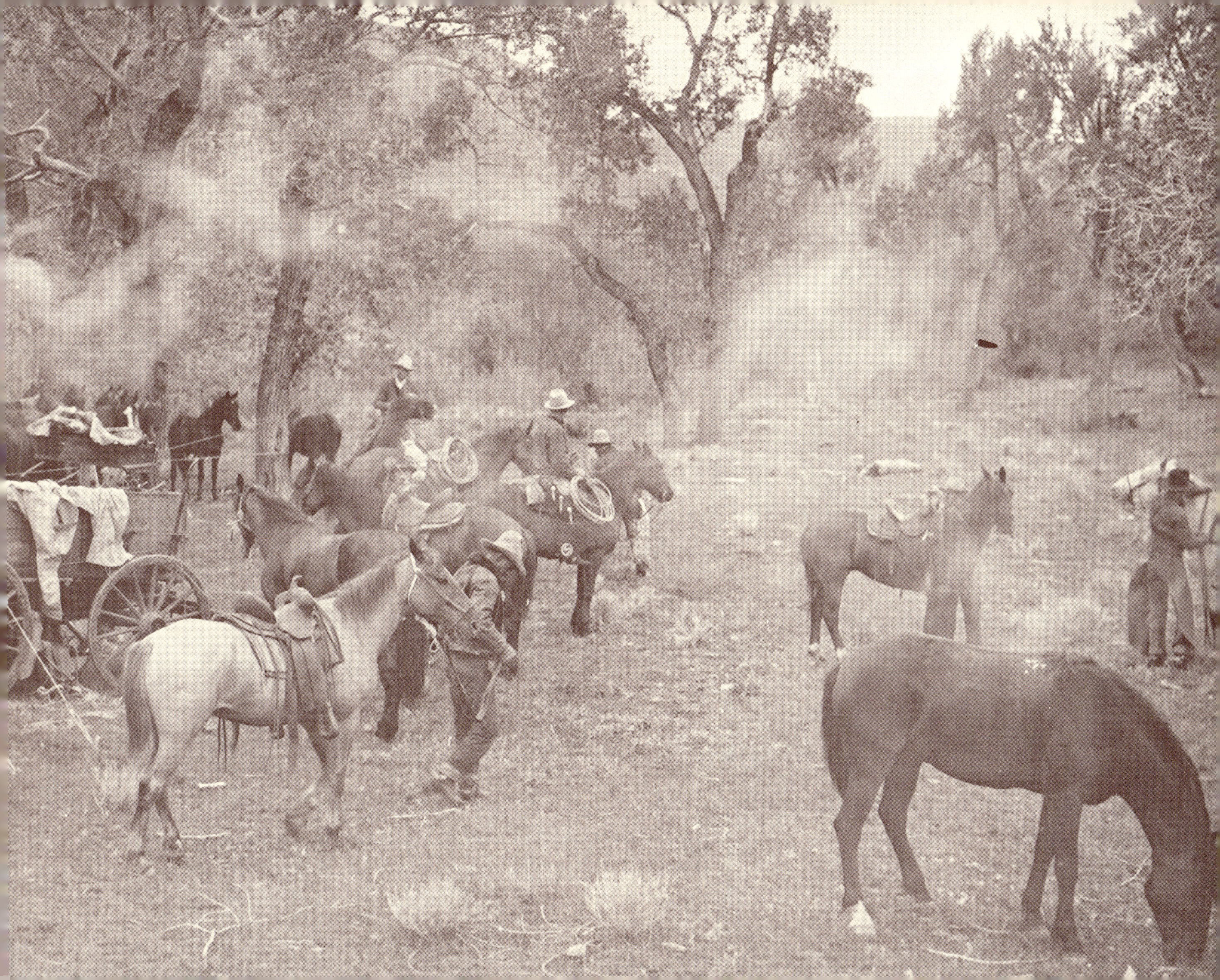

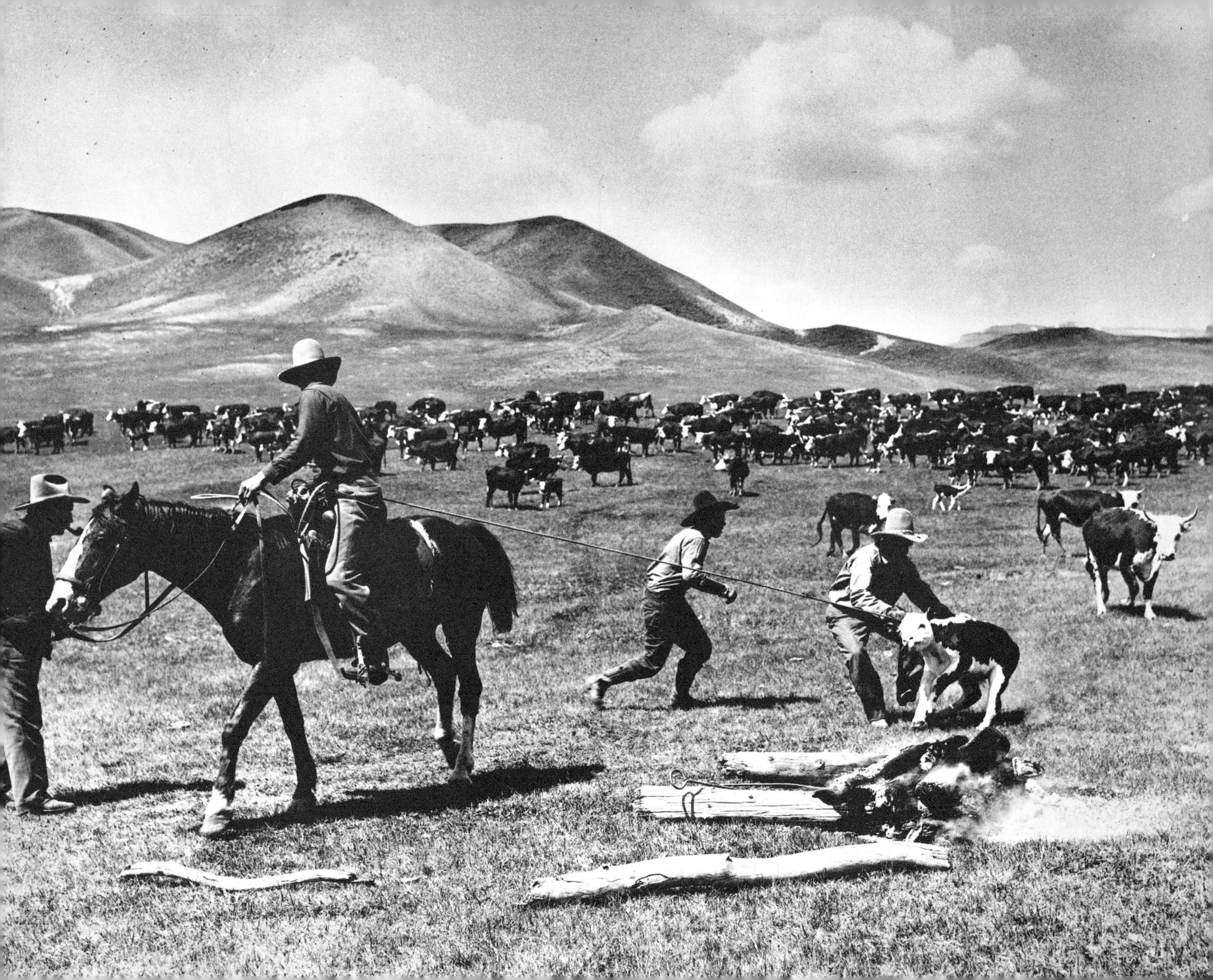

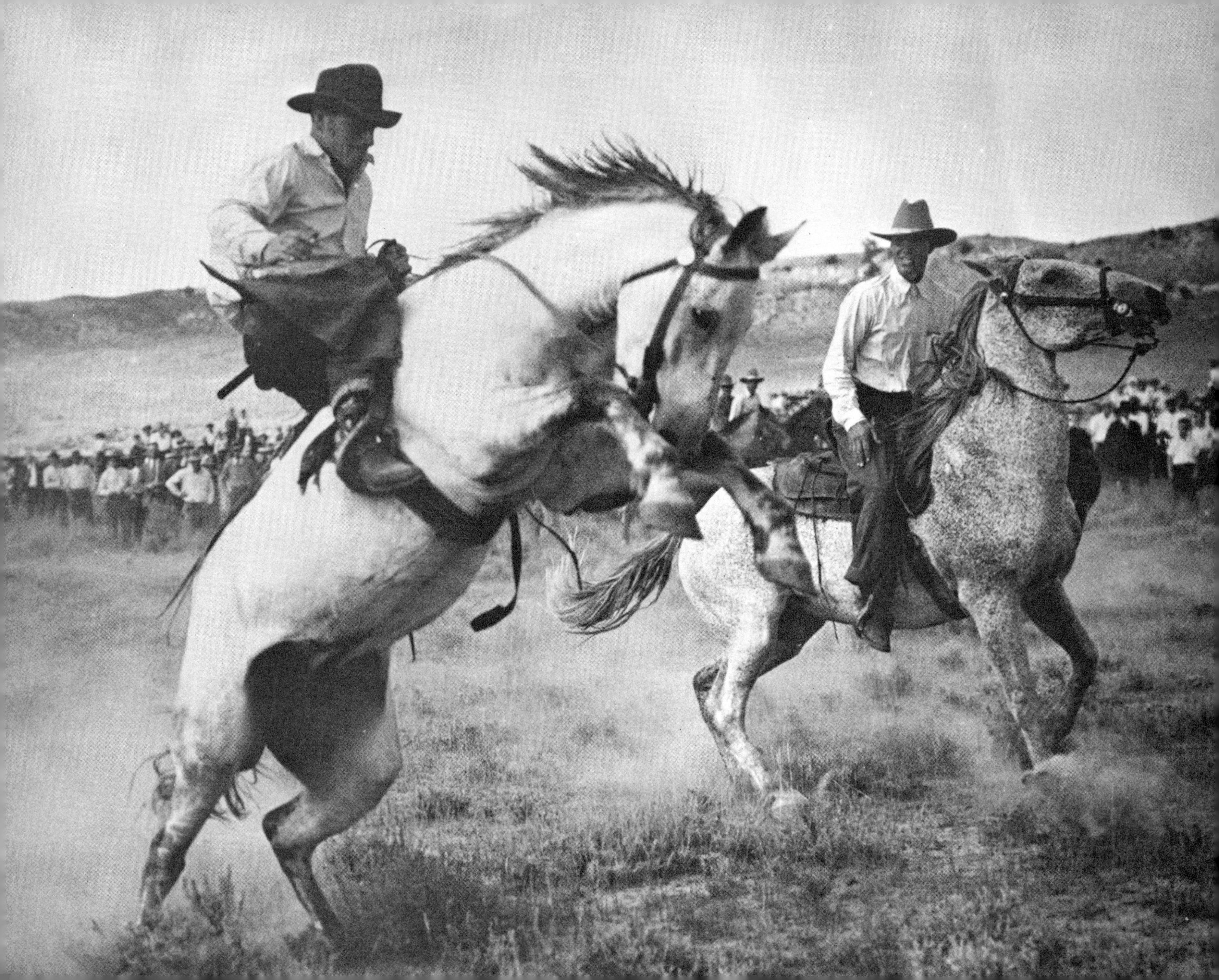

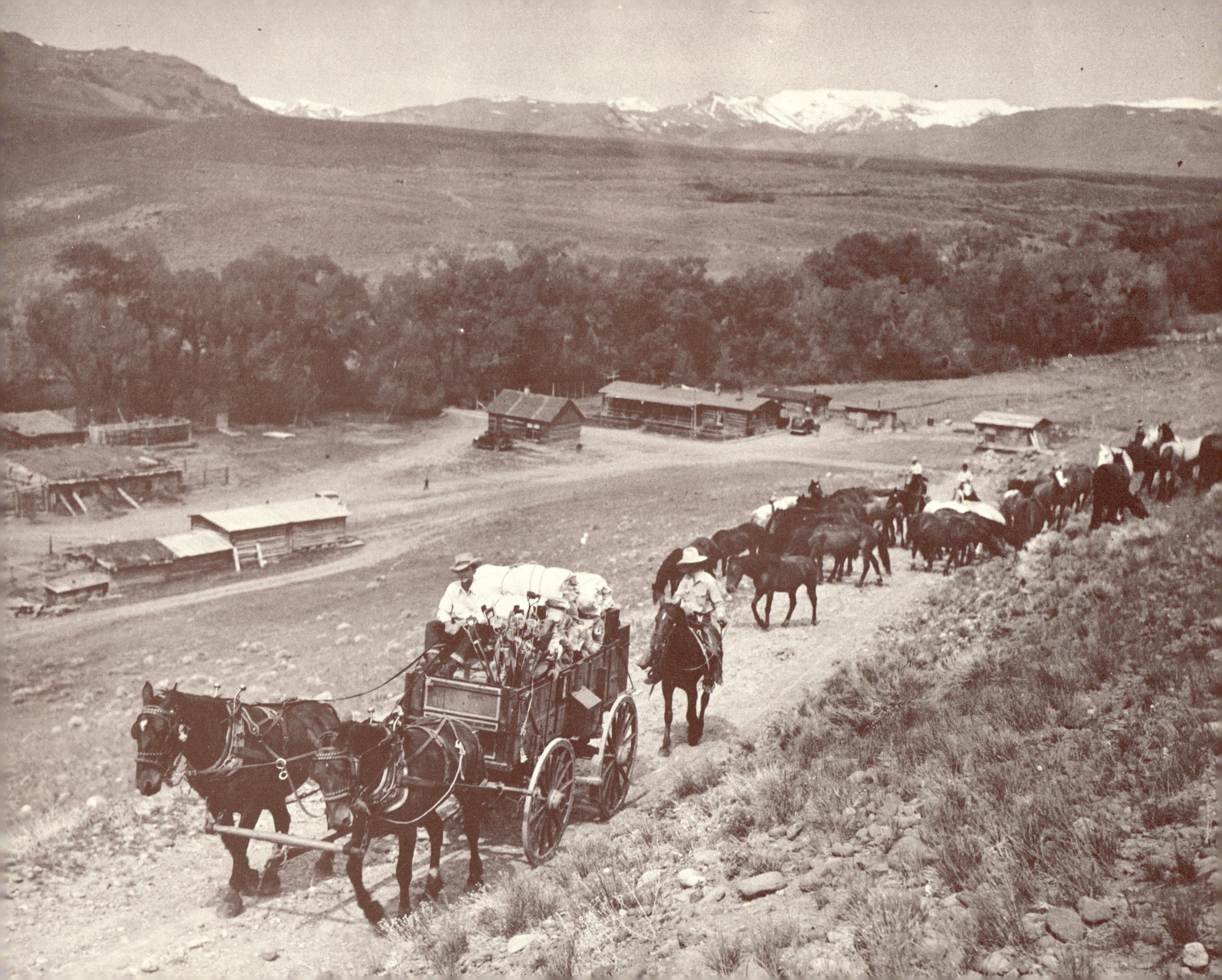

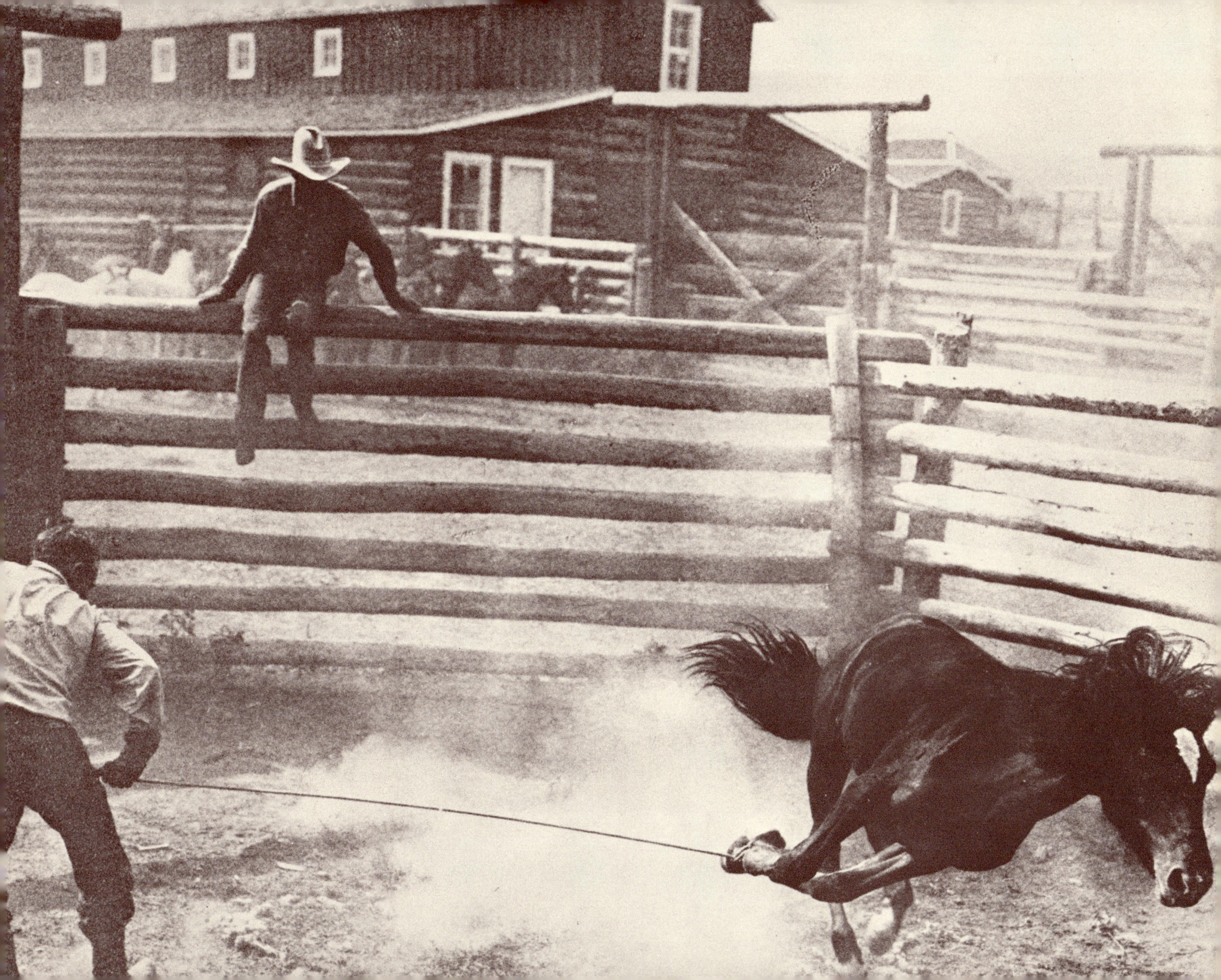

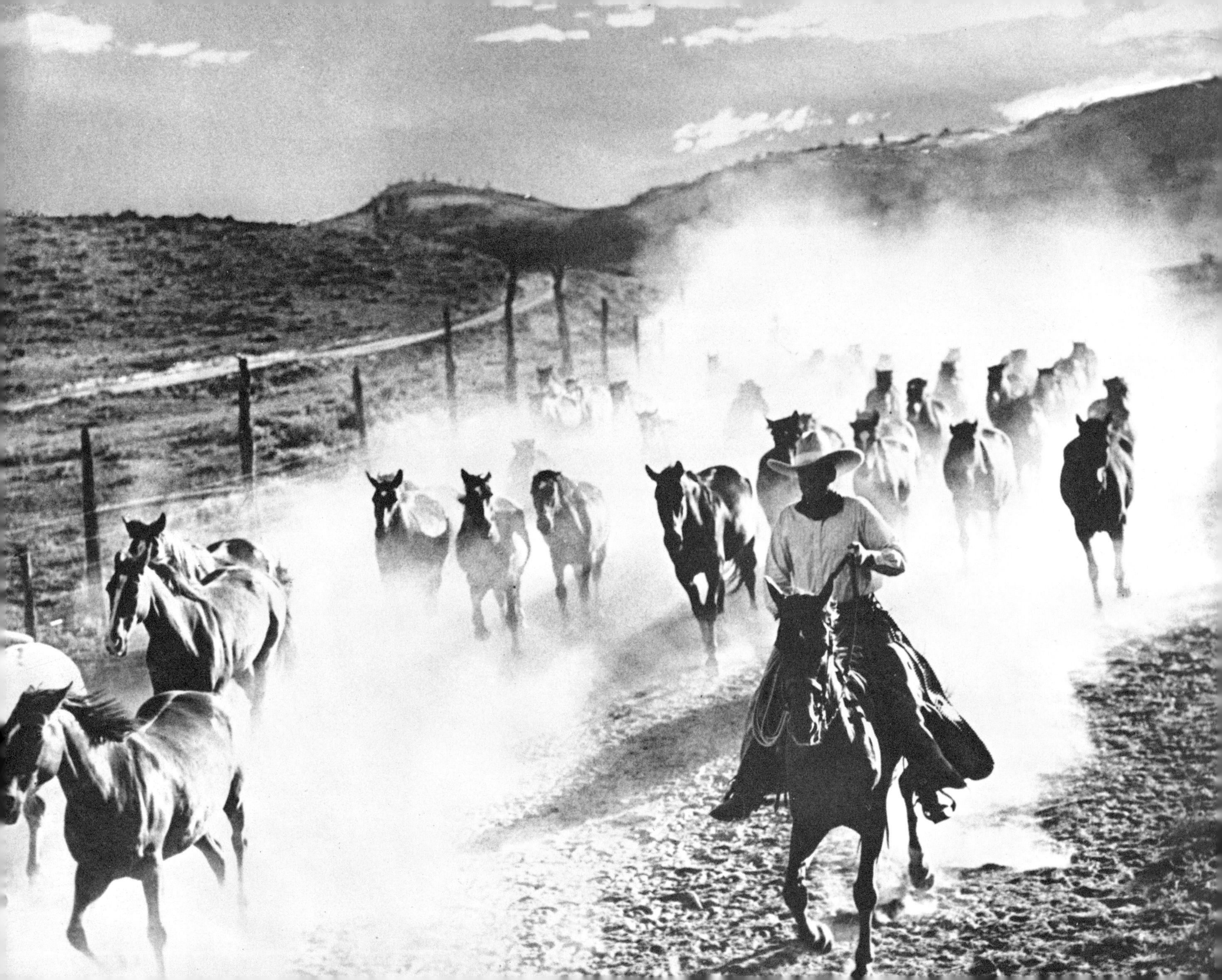

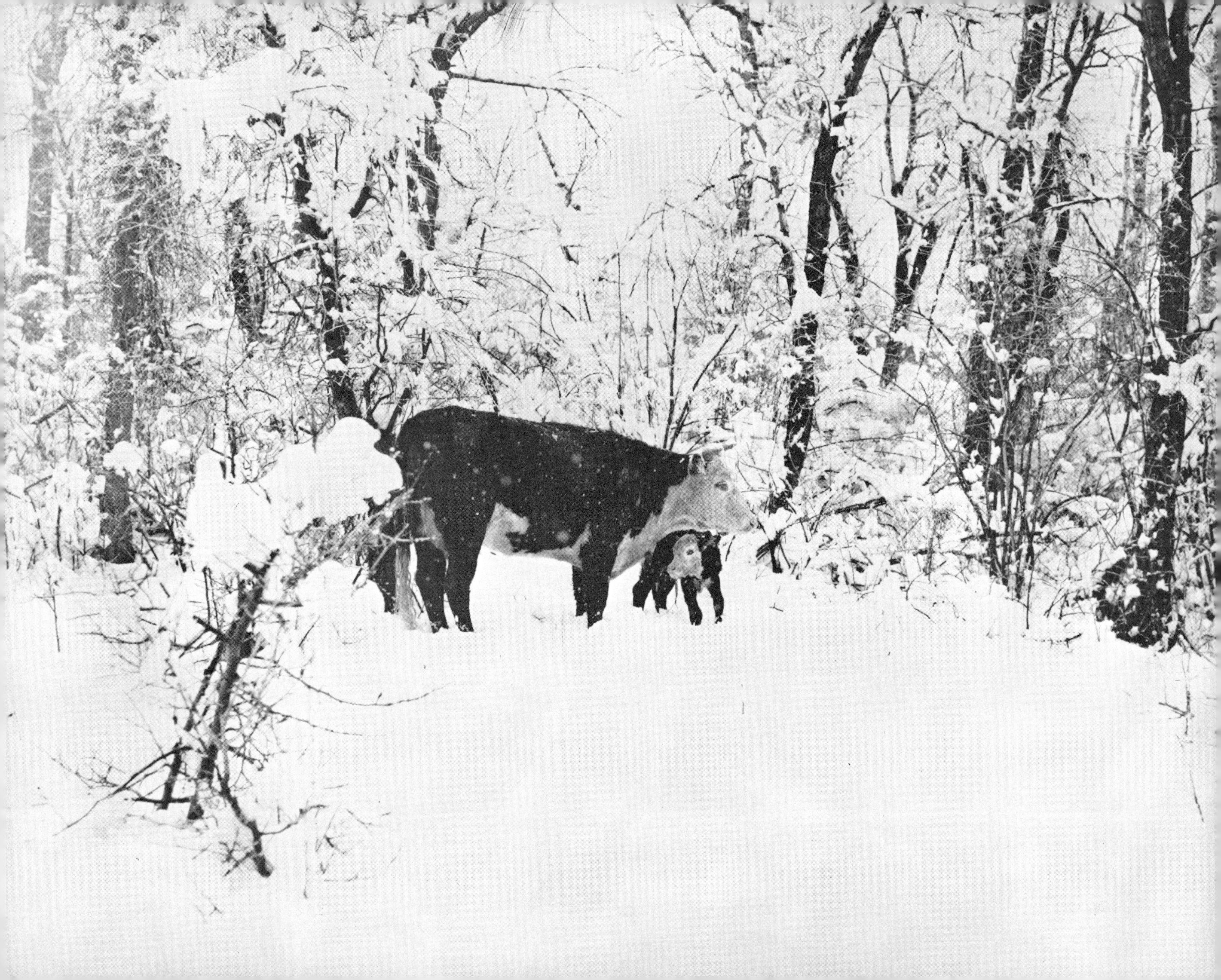

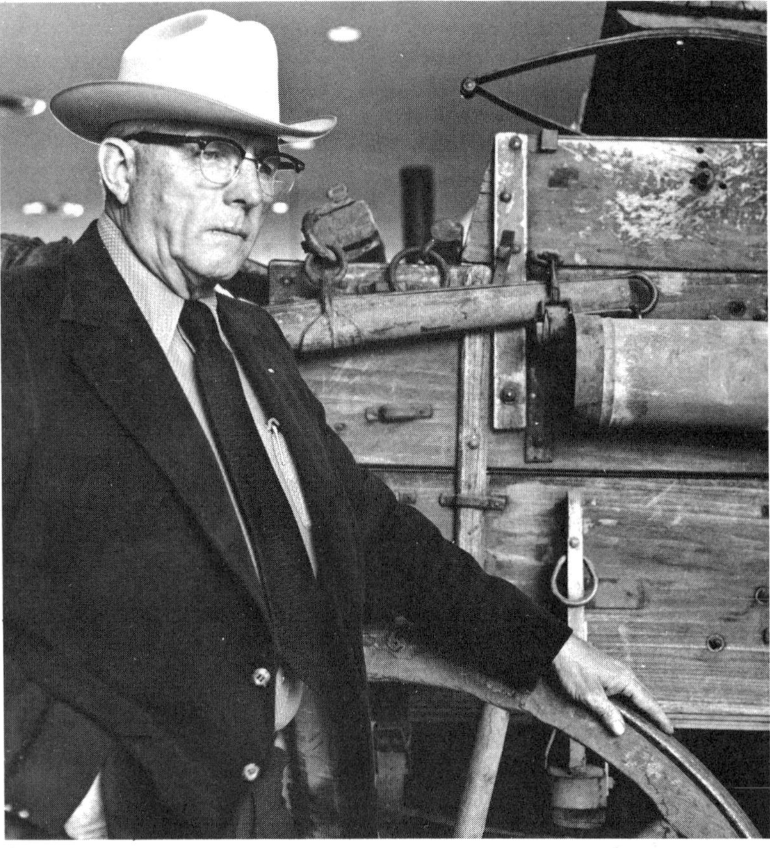

H. W. Willcutt

An important part of the Cowboy exhibition is the roundup camp which forms the central display. The items included in this portion of the exhibition are genuine. They have been loaned to us by H. W. Willcutt, of Muddy Creek Ranch, near Hardin, Montana.

Mr. Willcutt was born in 1909 at the little town of Rosebud, Montana on the south bank of the Yellowstone River. He has spent his entire life in the Montana ranch country. Mr. Willcutt is pure cowman through and through.

The traditions of the western range heritage are kept alive on the Muddy Creek. Mr. Willcutt has written down some of his background as well as the history of the roundup wagons utilized in the display:

"My exposure to a roundup wagon and cowboys began when I was nine months old in the early summer of 1910, when my parents moved to Lame Deer, Montana, on the Cheyenne Indian Reservation, and my father became Livestock Superintendent for the Cheyenne Indian Tribe. He was there in that capacity through the year 1913, then was transferred to Crow Agency, Montana to be Livestock Superintendent for the Crow Tribe and was there until the spring of 1917. That spring, he went to work as manager for the American Livestock and Loan Co., with headquarters at Eagle Springs, nine miles south of Hardin, Montana, on the Crow Reservation, west side of the Big Horn River. He was there from 1917 to the spring of 1924 when Mr. E. L. Dana took over the lease from the American Livestock and Loan Co. and started an outfit of his own. My father continued on with Mr. Dana as manager until 1936, when Mr. Dana sold out to a Mr. Charlie Miller. During this period of years with Mr. Dana, the outfit controlled 1,000,000 acres of grazing land on the Crow Indian Reservation and in Wyoming, from the state line at Pass Creek to Dayton, Wyoming. They ran 30,000 cattle and at times had two roundup wagons going at the same time. So growing up around the Cheyenne wagon, the Crow ID wagon, The American Livestock & Loan Co. and Dana wagons and on down to the time of our own wagon, known as the Mill Iron (⚊○⚊), I have had almost a lifetime exposure to what a roundup wagon is used for.

I started out in a very small way in 1929, hoping that someday I might be the owner of a good sized ranch and this became a reality the spring of 1938, when my father and I became the owners of the Grapevine Ranch and 160,000 acres of Crow Indian leased land, which we ran up to 8,000 head of cattle until 1951, when we sold some of the range and cut the cattle down in numbers and again in the fall of 1967, we sold the Grapevine Ranch and some of the range land along with some more cattle, which cut our operation down to where we no longer had use for the roundup wagon.

In 1968, we built a complete new set of ranch buildings on Muddy Creek, our present location, and retired the roundup wagon to the inside of a new Butler building, using it only on occasions for fun time.

This wagon was made up by me in the year 1938 and according to the way I thought it should be equipped, using my lifetime experience around one. The only thing I used off another wagon, which was from the old Dana wagon, are the bolster springs."

Mr. Willcutt's roundup camp adds a vital dimension to our Cowboy exhibition. The old cowpunchers who knew these wagons as home during the roundup seasons of long ago would be surprised . . . and we hope pleased, to see them displayed within the walls of a museum dedicated to the memory of the Old West.

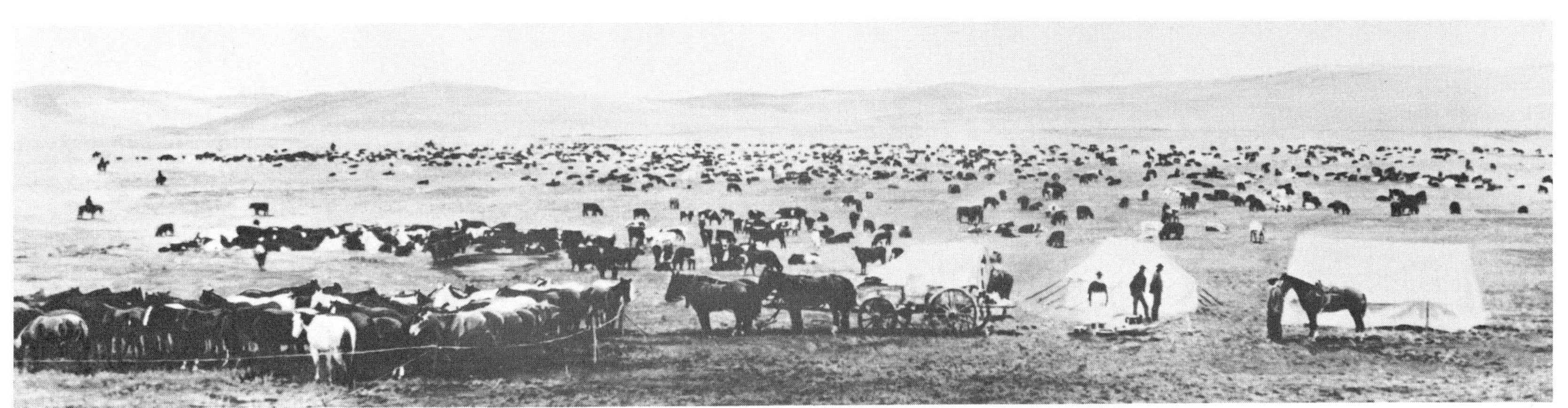

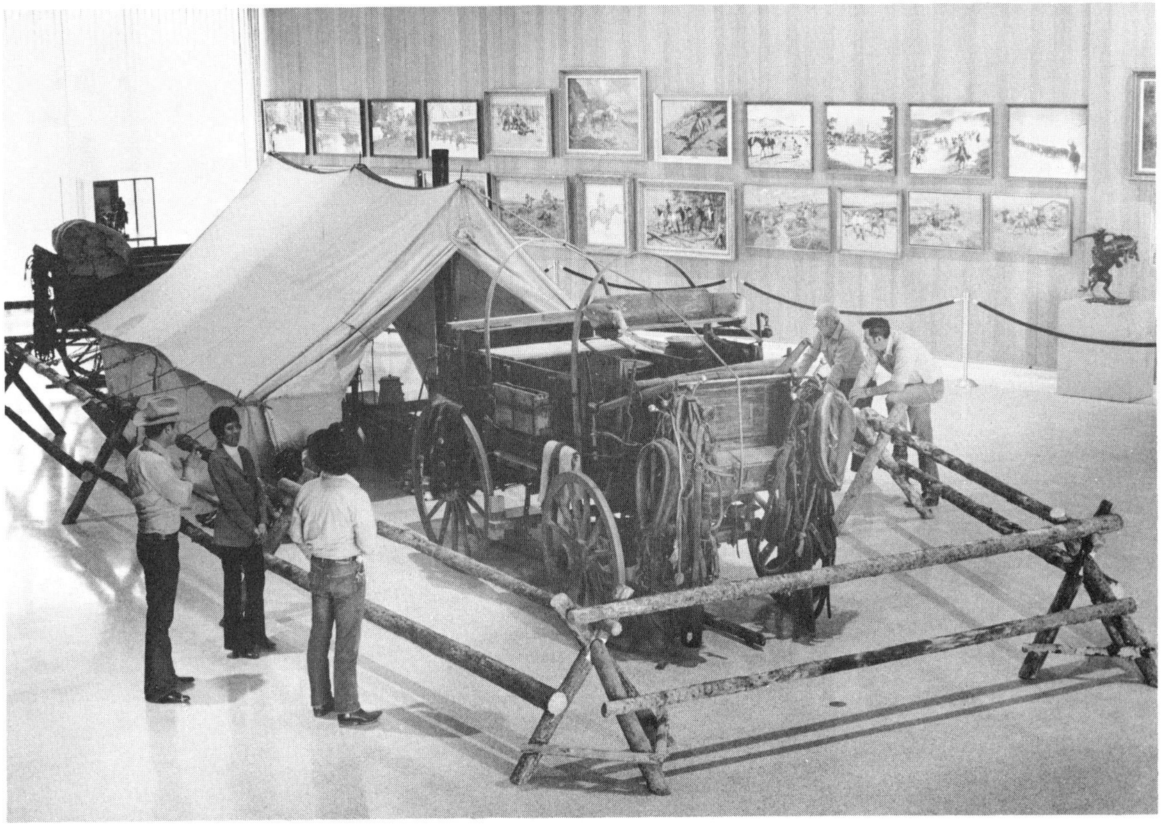

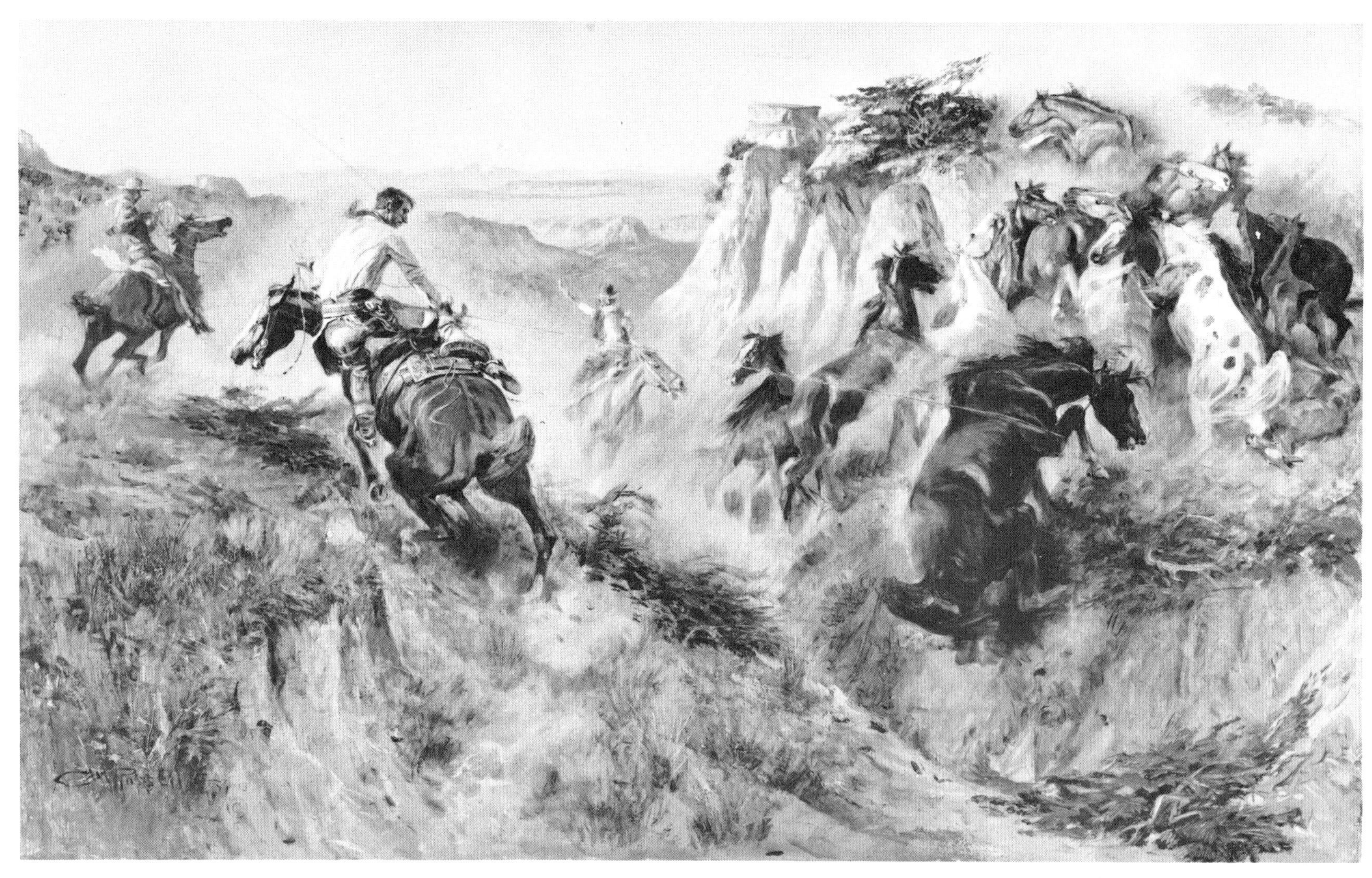

THE WILD HORSE HUNTERS, Charles M. Russell, oil, 30⅛"x47"
Lent by Amon Carter Museum, Fort Worth, Texas

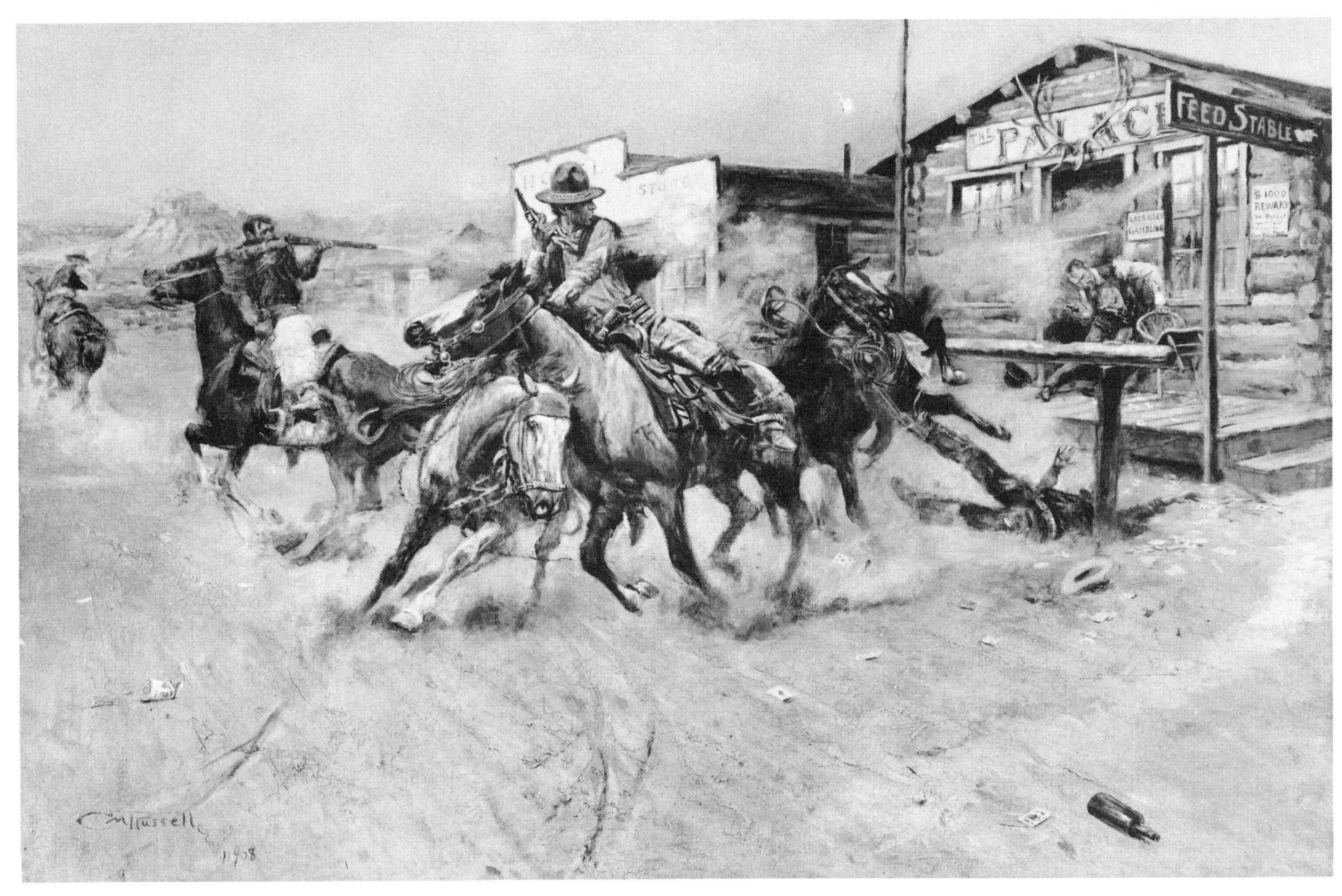

SMOKE OF A .45, Charles M. Russell, oil, 24¼"x36"
Lent by Amon Carter Museum, Fort Worth, Texas

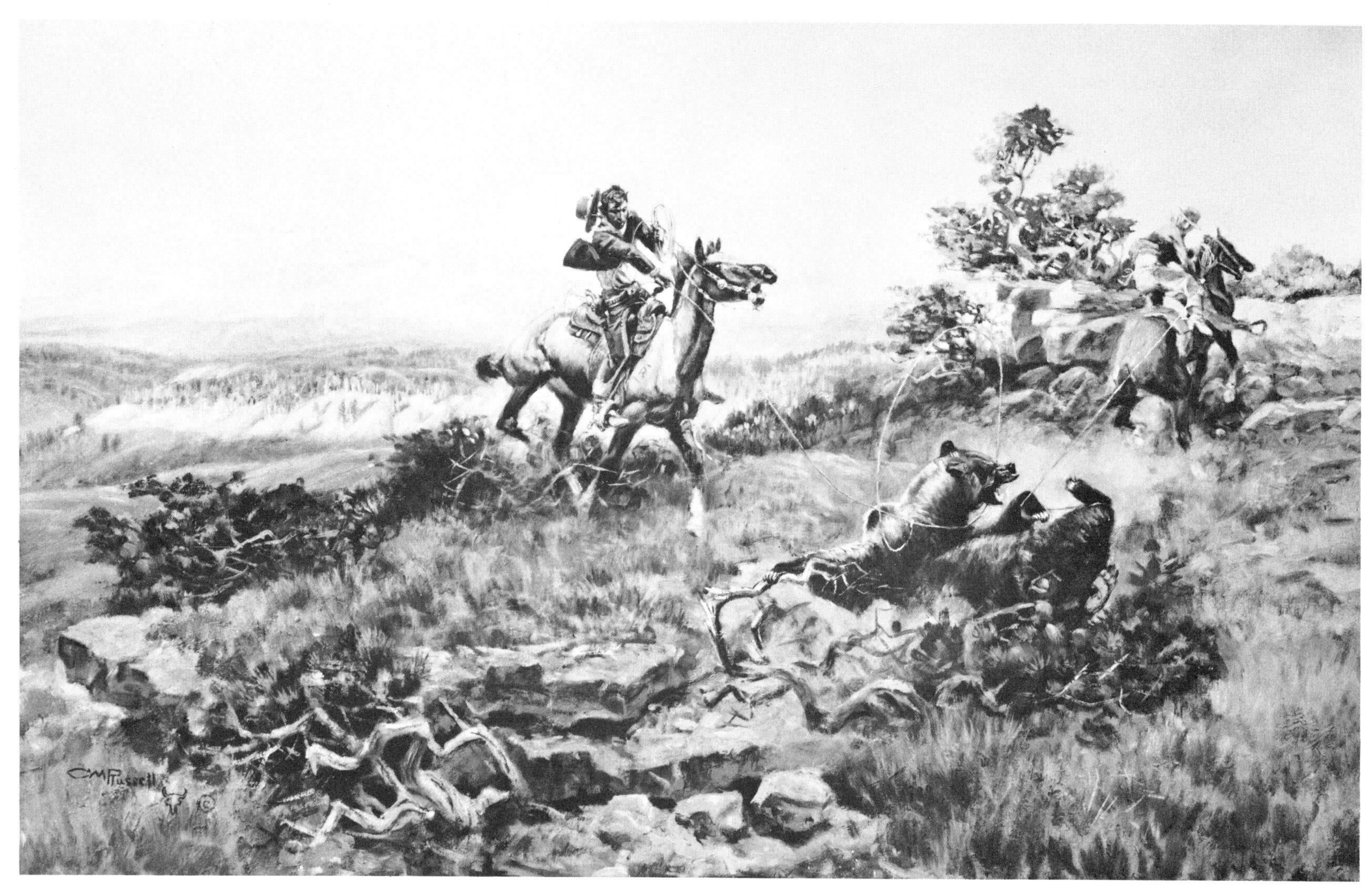

THE STRANGLERS, Charles M. Russell, oil, 30"x48"
The William E. Weiss Collection in the Whitney Gallery of Western Art

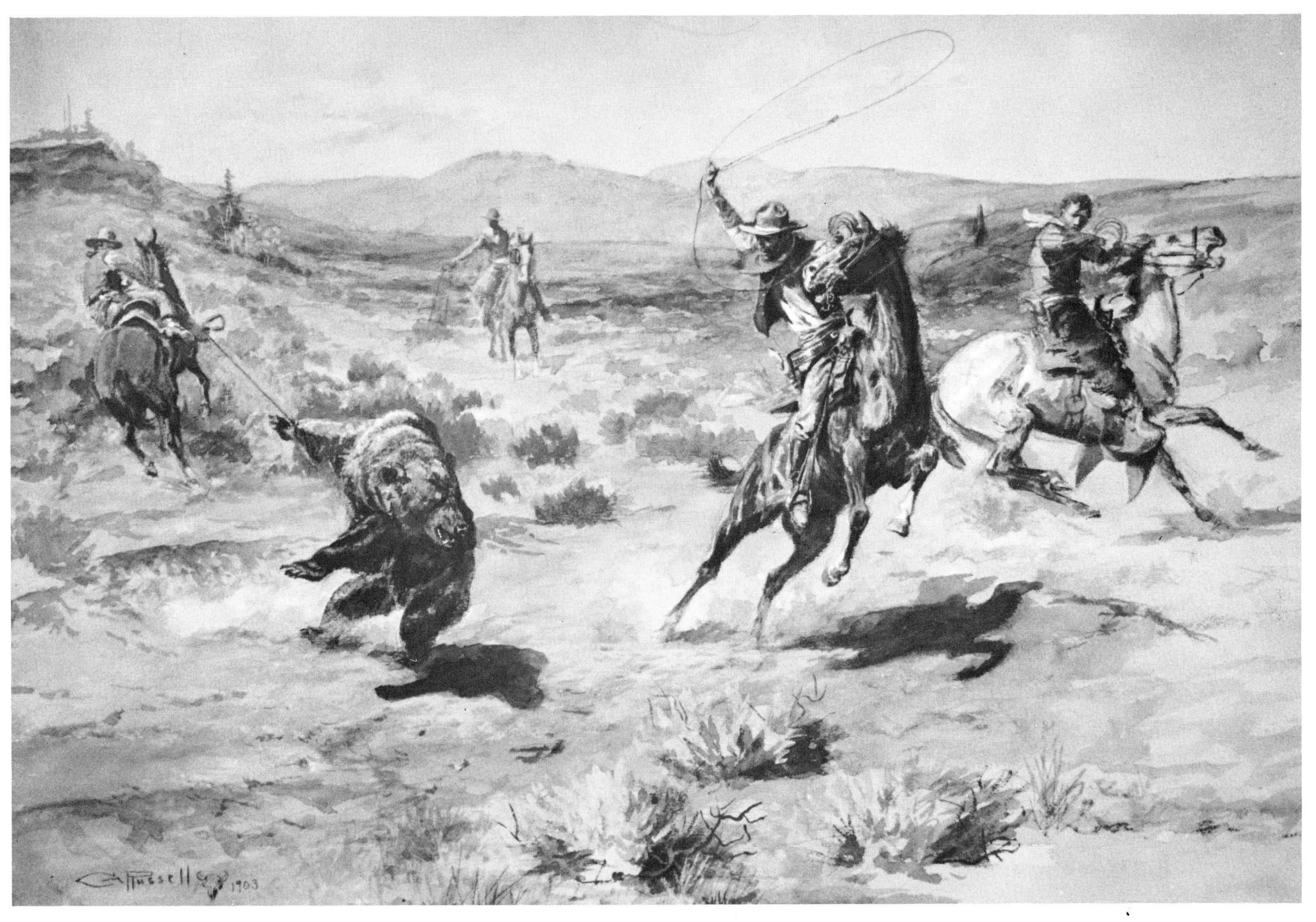

ROPING A GRIZZLY, Charles M. Russell, watercolor, 19¾"x28¾"
Permanent Collection of the Whitney Gallery of Western Art

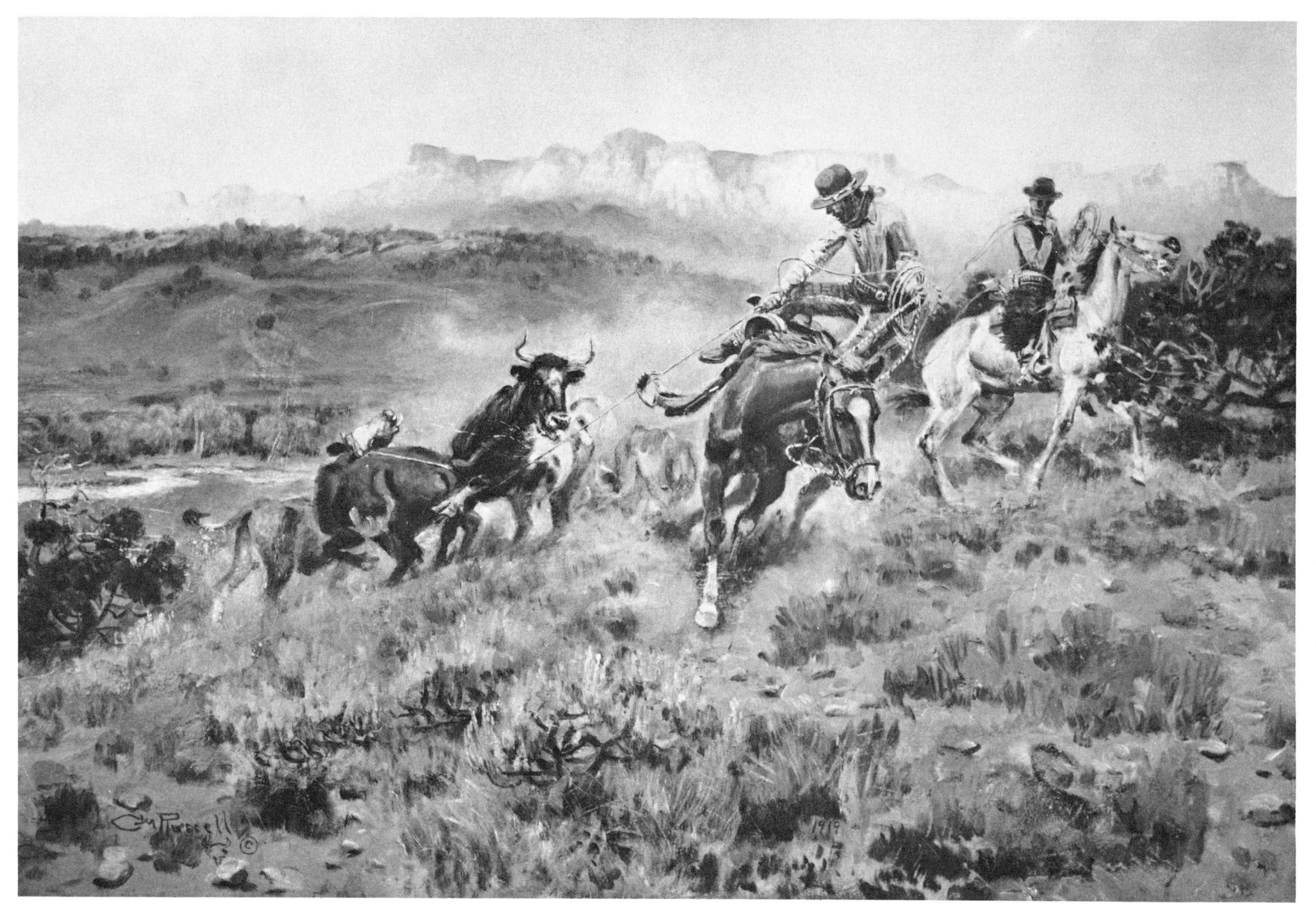

ROUNDUP ON THE MUSSELSHELL, Charles M. Russell, oil, 24"x36"
The William E. Weiss Collection in the Whitney Gallery of Western Art

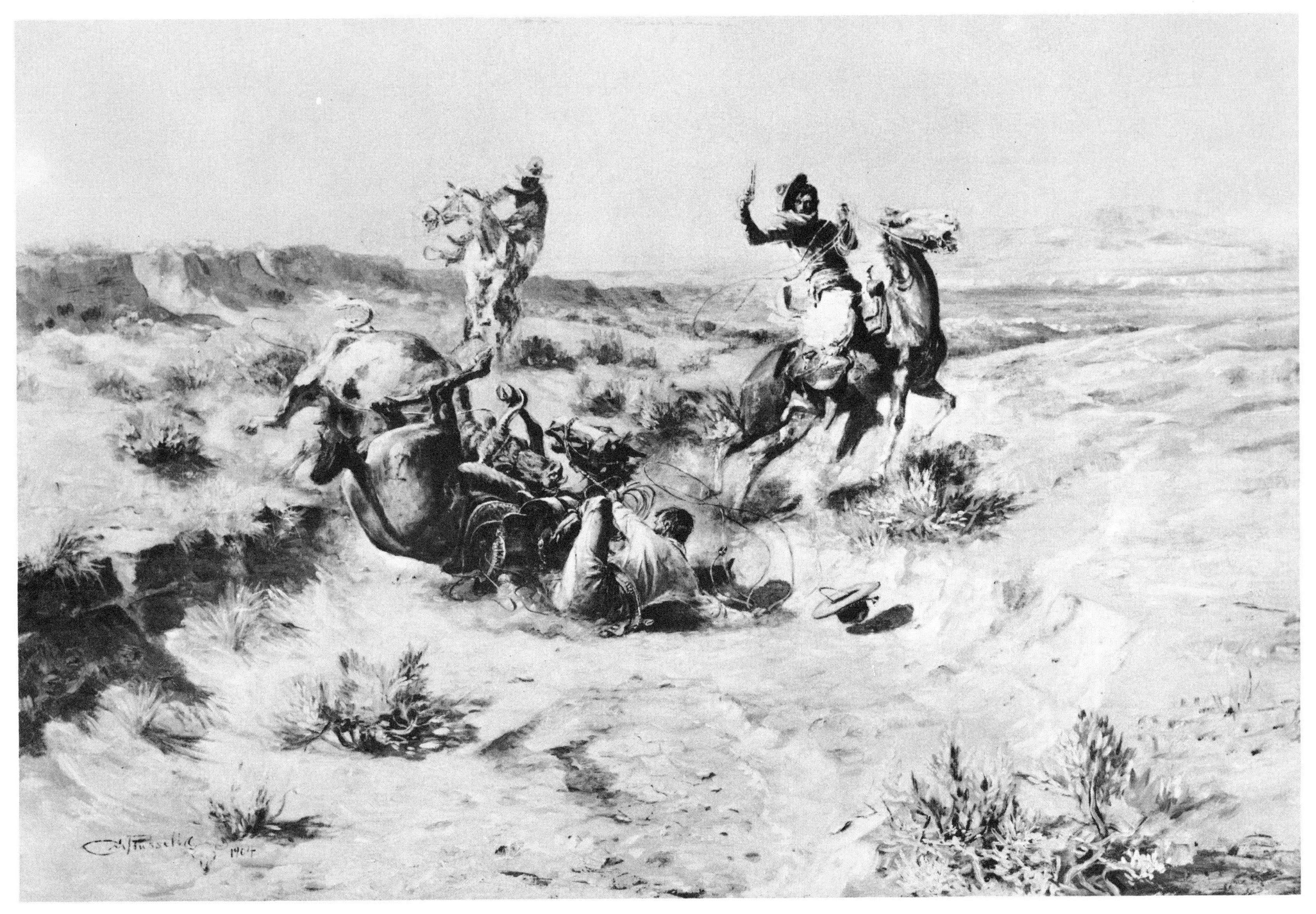

BROKEN ROPE, Charles M. Russell, oil, 24"x36⅛"
Lent by Amon Carter Museum, Fort Worth, Texas

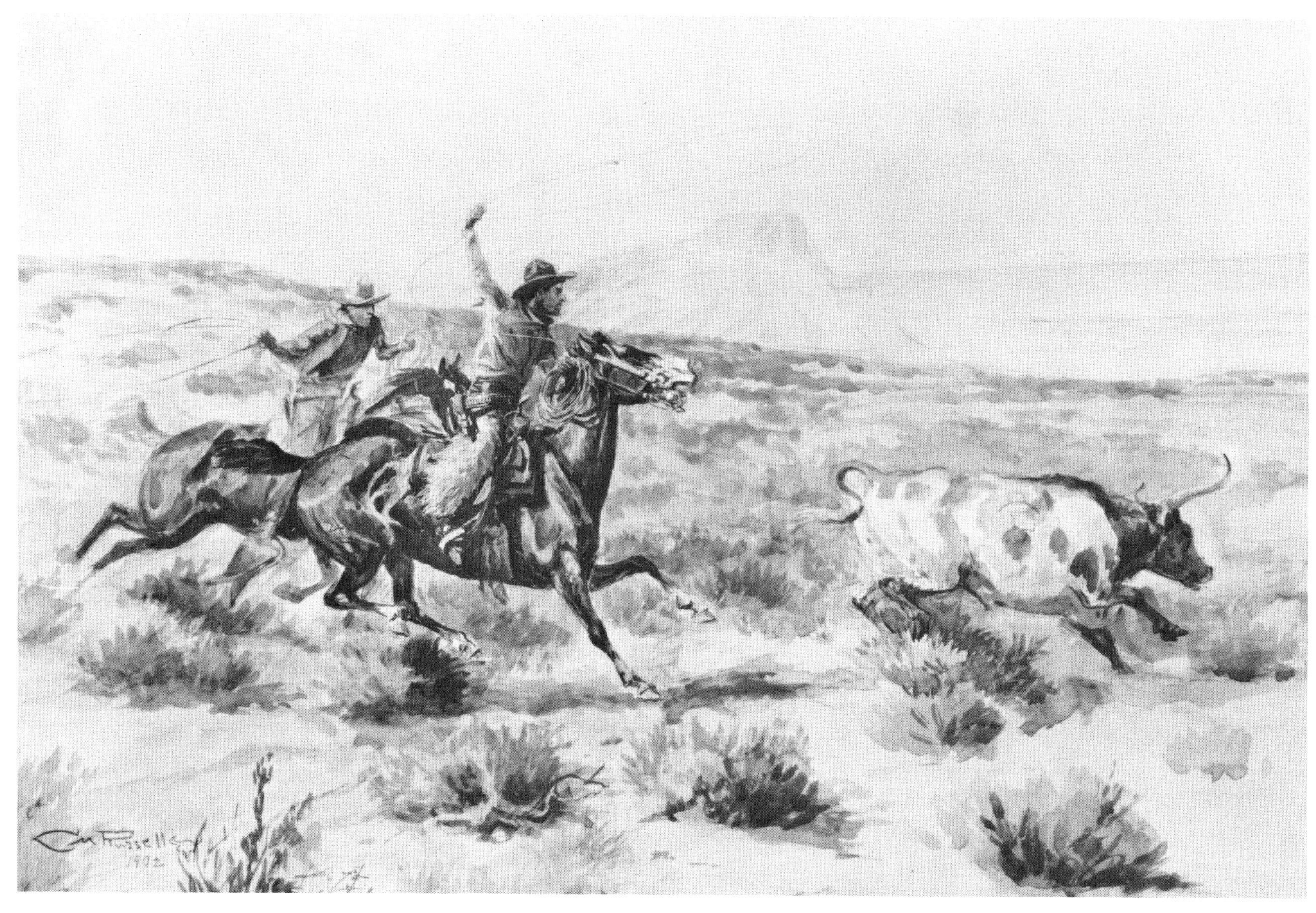

ROPING A STEER, Charles M. Russell, watercolor, 14"x21"
Lent by William J. Williams Family

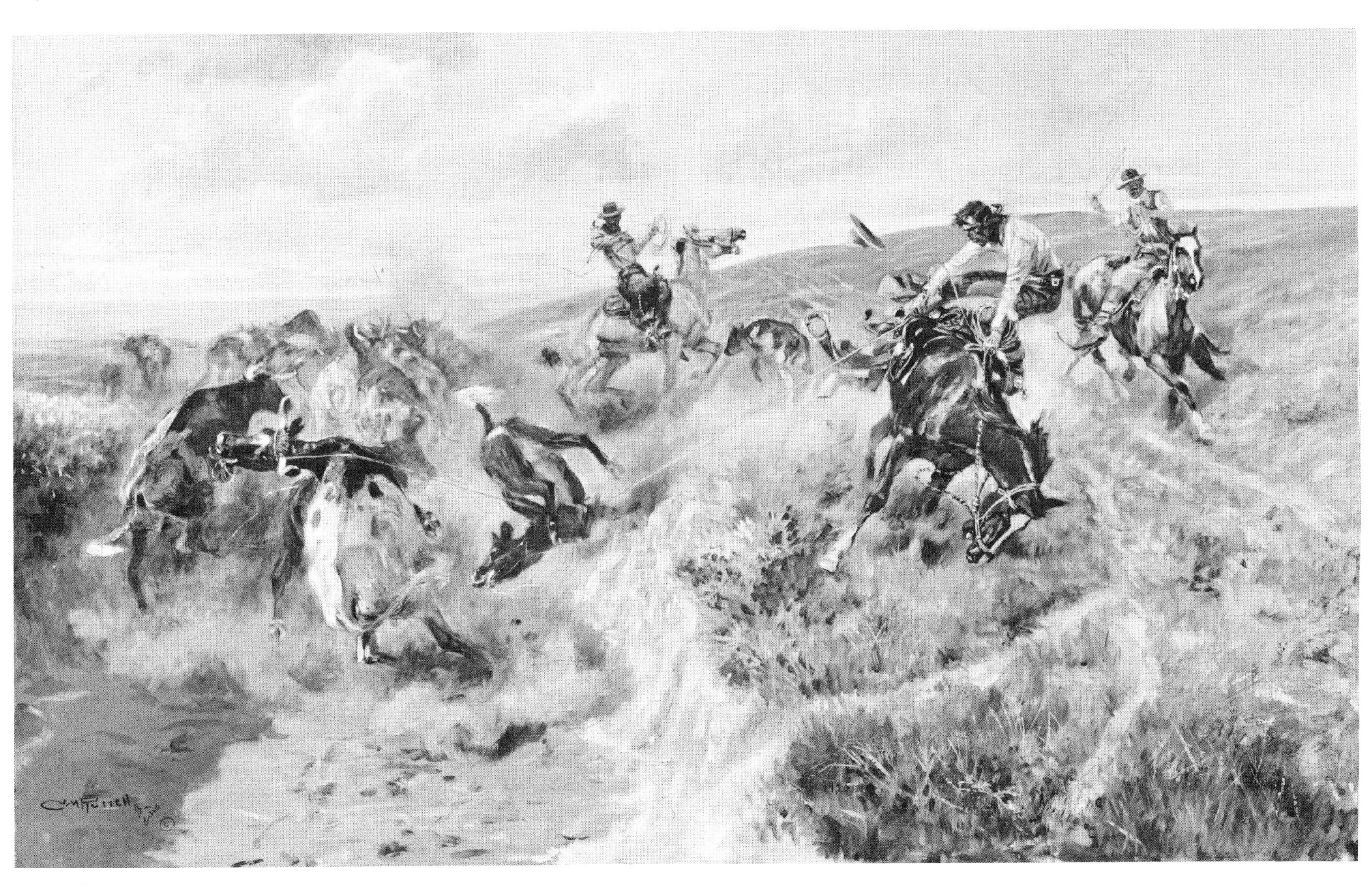

A TIGHT DALLY AND A LOOSE LATIGO, Charles M. Russell, oil, 30"x48"
Lent by Amon Carter Museum, Fort Worth, Texas

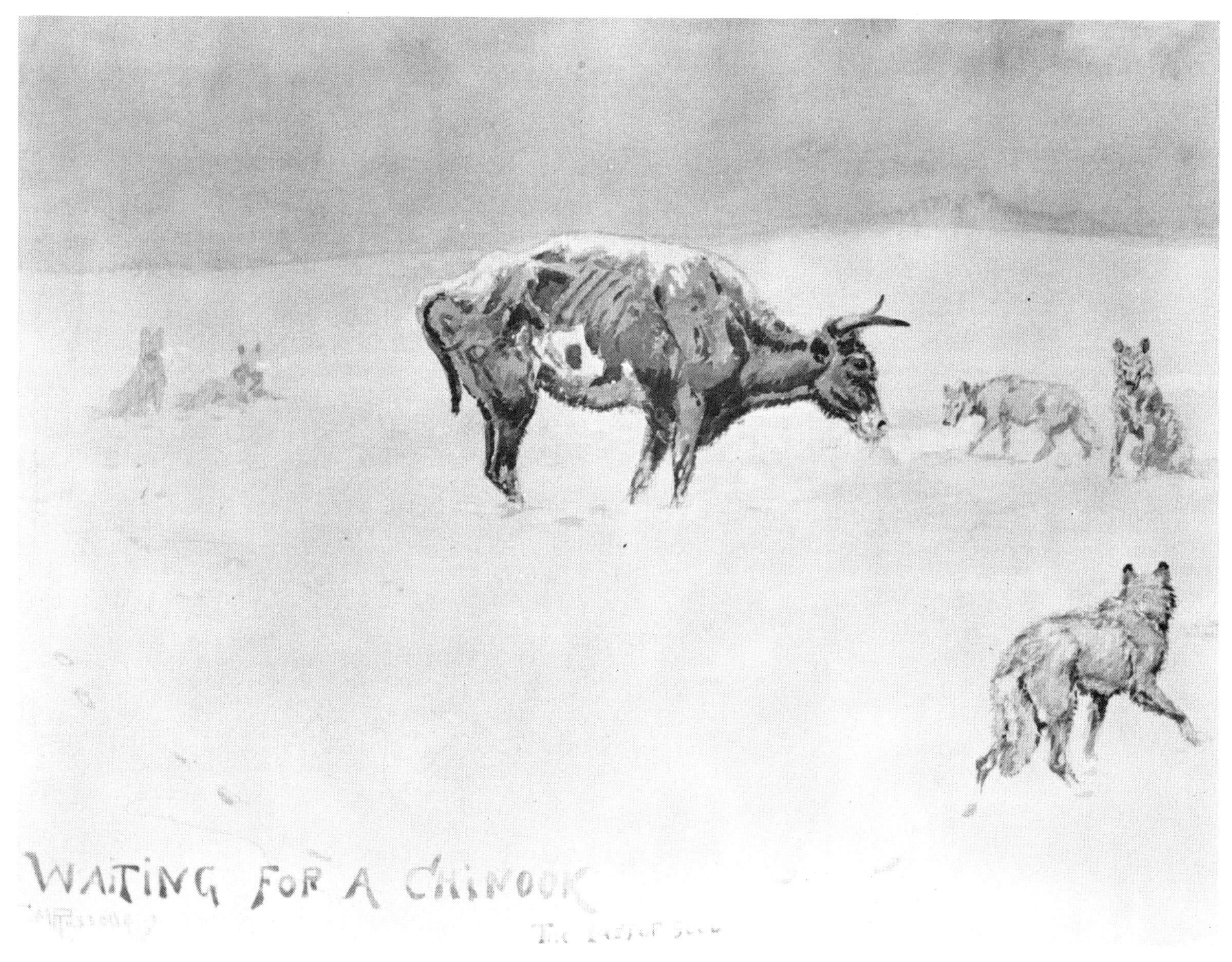

WAITING FOR A CHINOOK, Charles M. Russell, watercolor, 20"x29"
Permanent Collection of the Whitney Gallery of Western Art

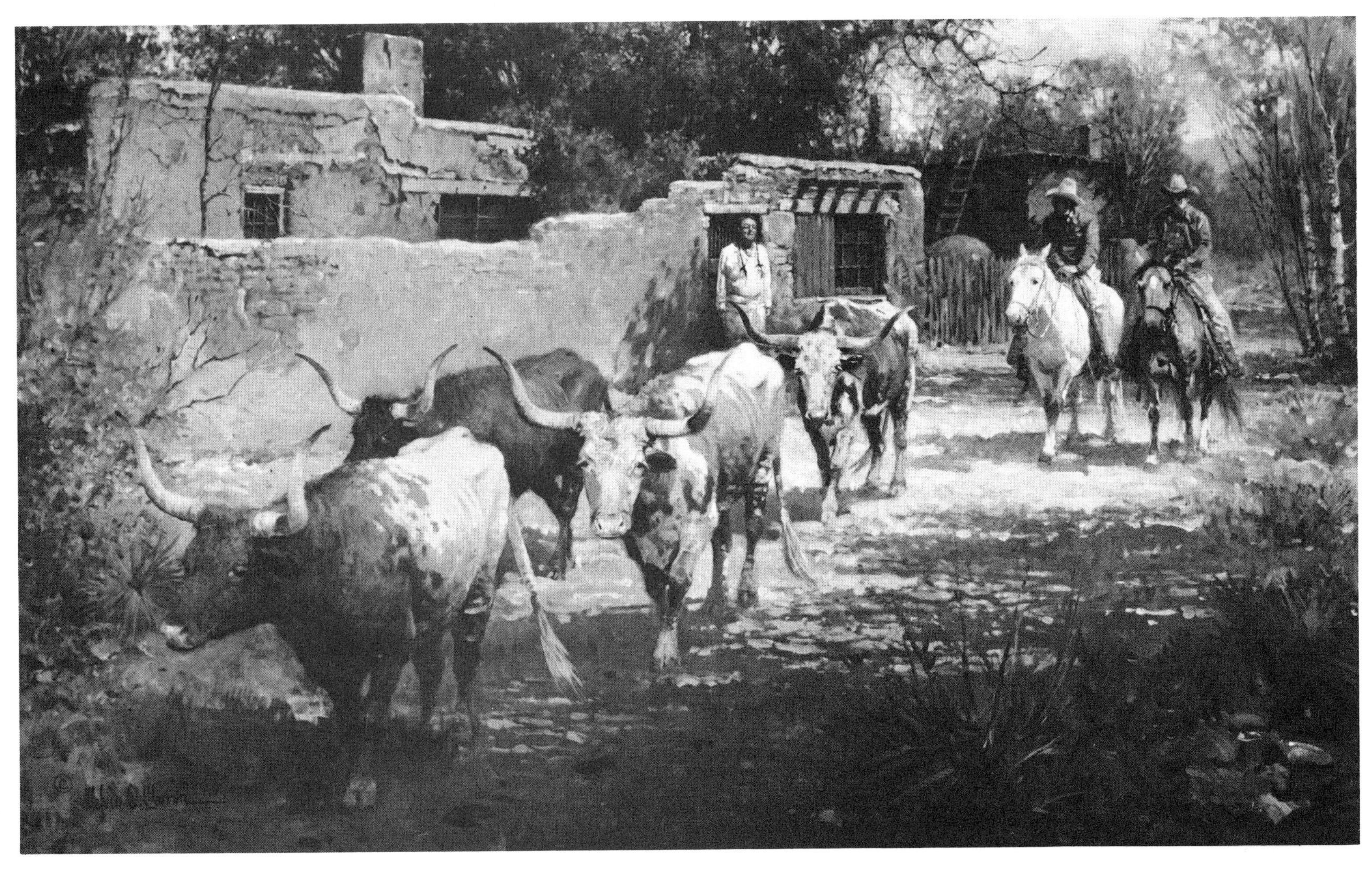

REMNANTS OF THE HERD, Melvin Warren, oil, 36"x60"
Lent by Mr. and Mrs. Robert K. Hillin

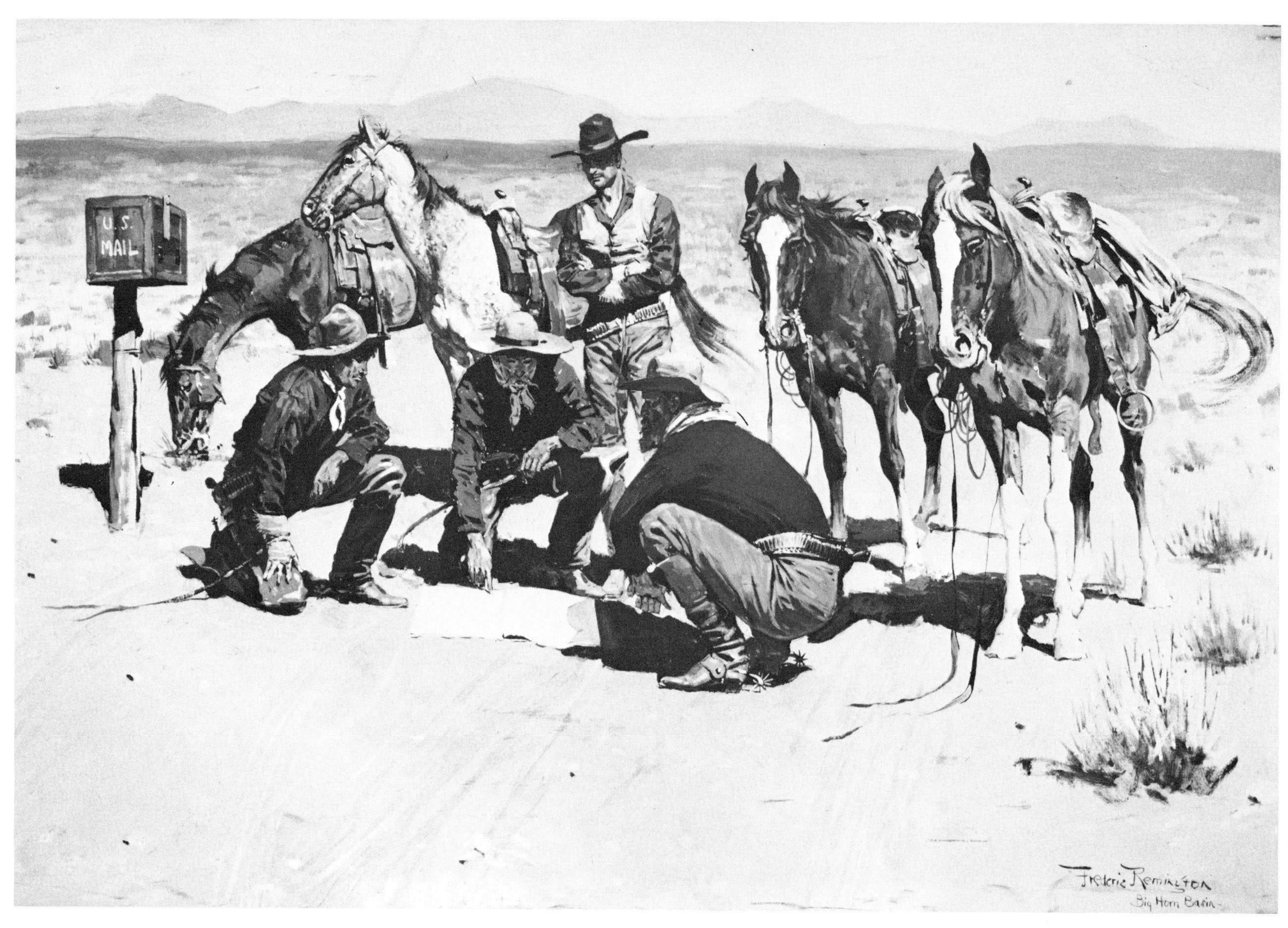

POST OFFICE IN THE COW COUNTRY, Frederic Remington, oil, 27"x40"
Lent by Mr. William Magee

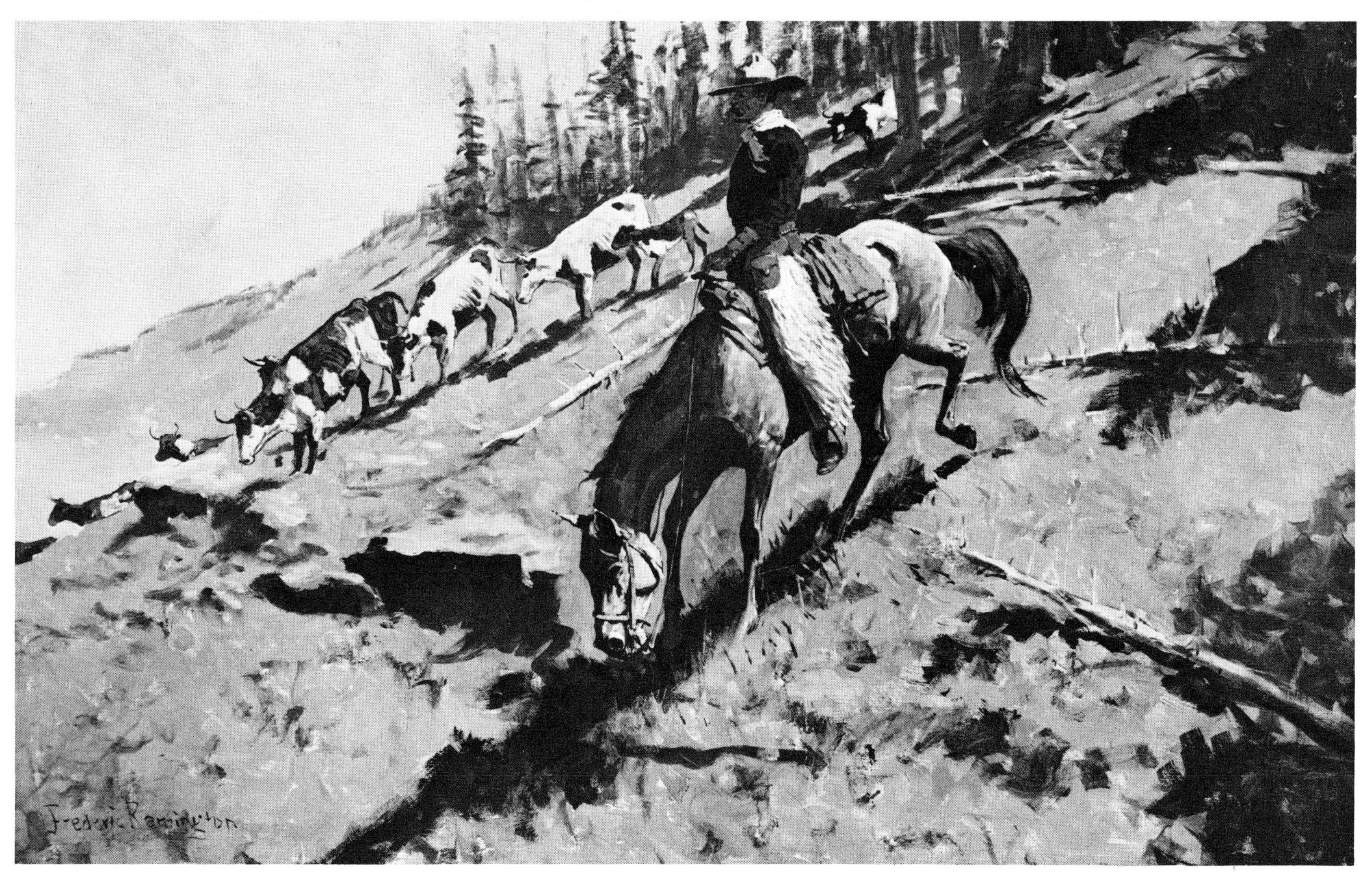

ROUNDUP, Frederic Remington, oil, 27"x40"
Permanent Collection of the Whitney Gallery of Western Art

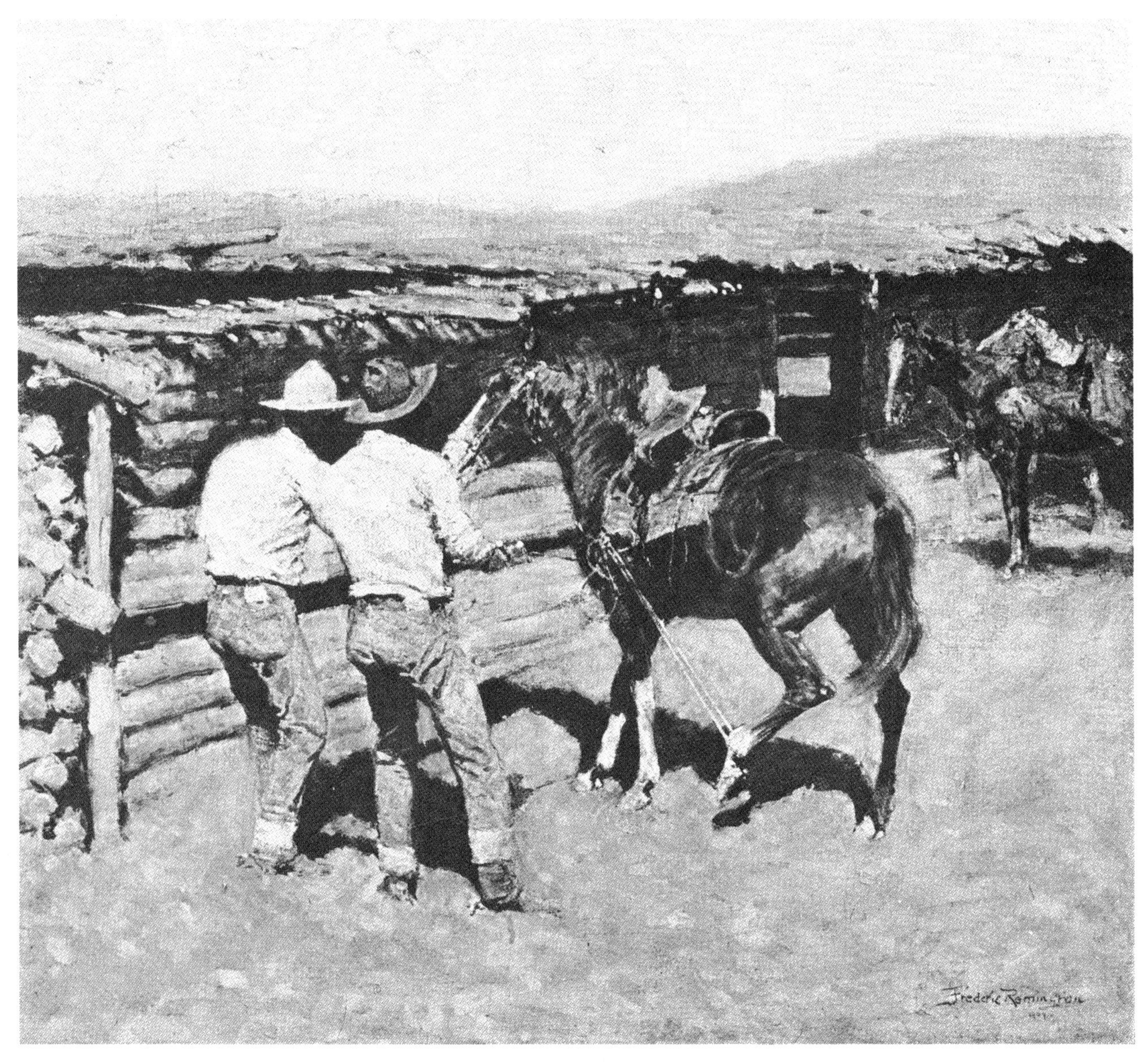

WAR BRIDLE, Frederic Remington, oil, 27"x40"
Lent Anonymously

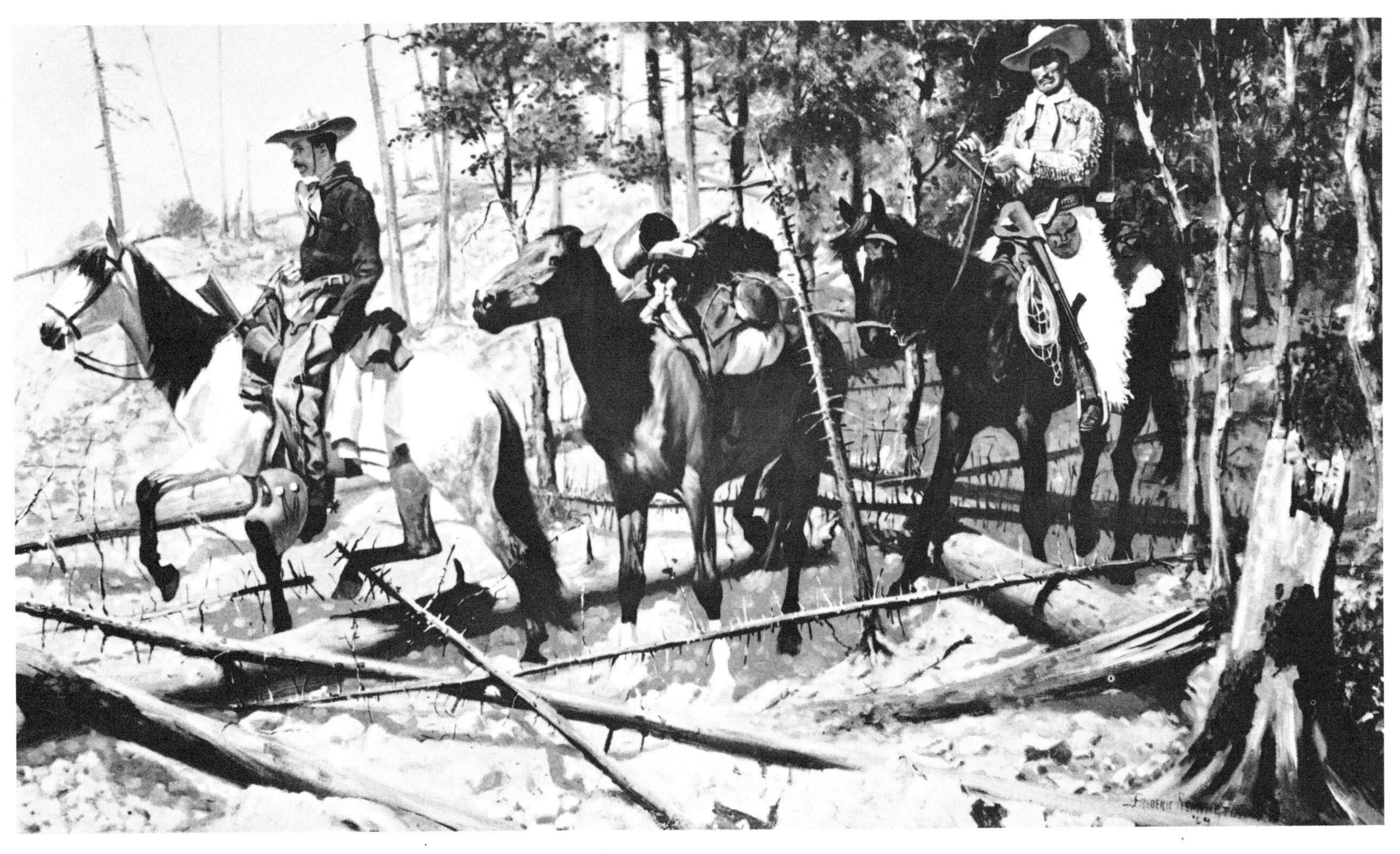

PROSPECTING FOR CATTLE RANGE, Frederic Remington, oil, 29"x50"
Permanent Collection of the Whitney Gallery of Western Art

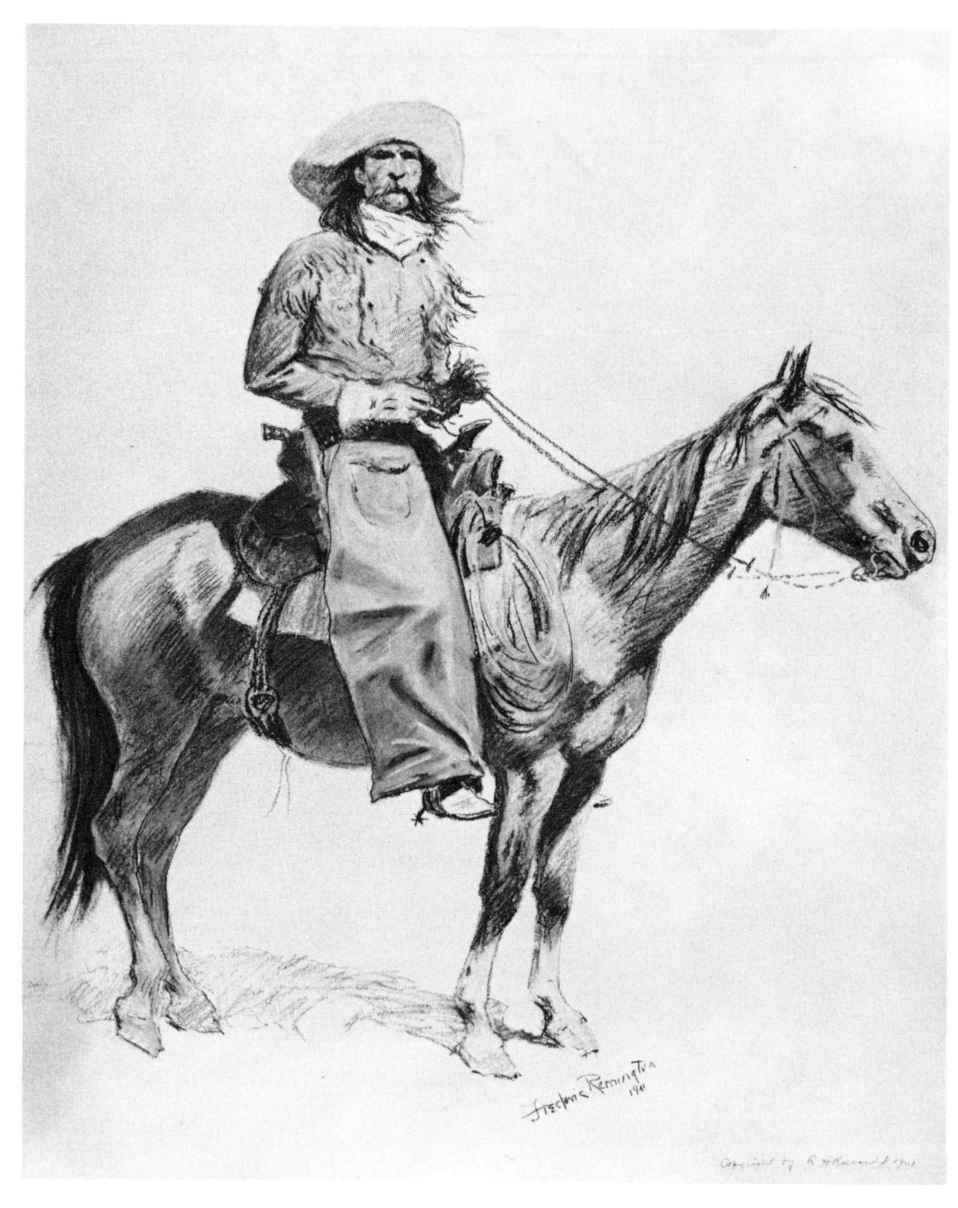

ARIZONA COWBOY, Frederic Remington, pastel, 27"x22"
Lent by Rockwell Foundation, Corning, New York

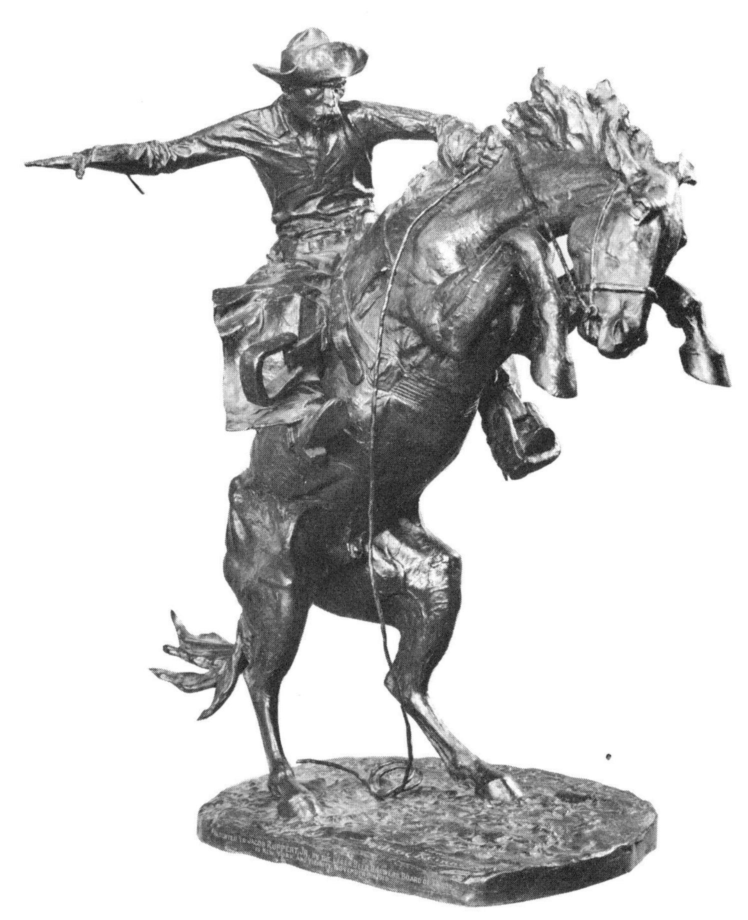

BRONCO BUSTER, Frederic Remington, bronze, Cast No. 10
Permanent Collection of the Whitney Gallery of Western Art

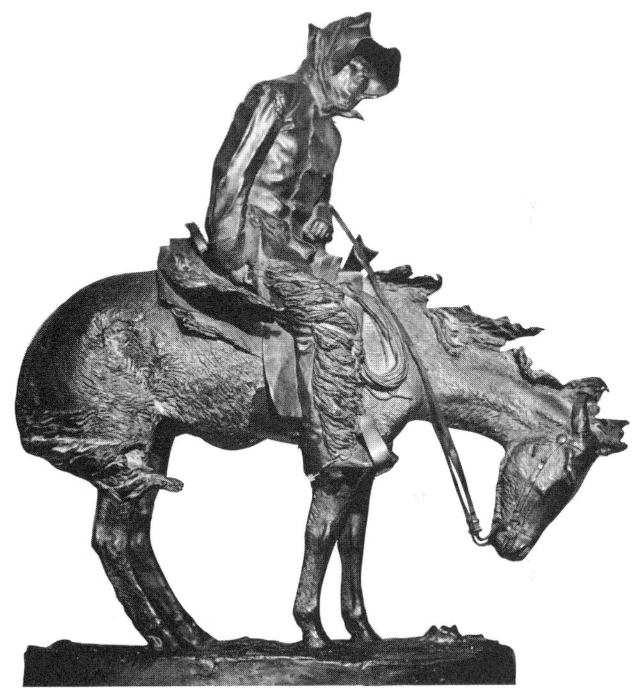

THE NORTHER, Frederic Remington, bronze
Lent Anonymously

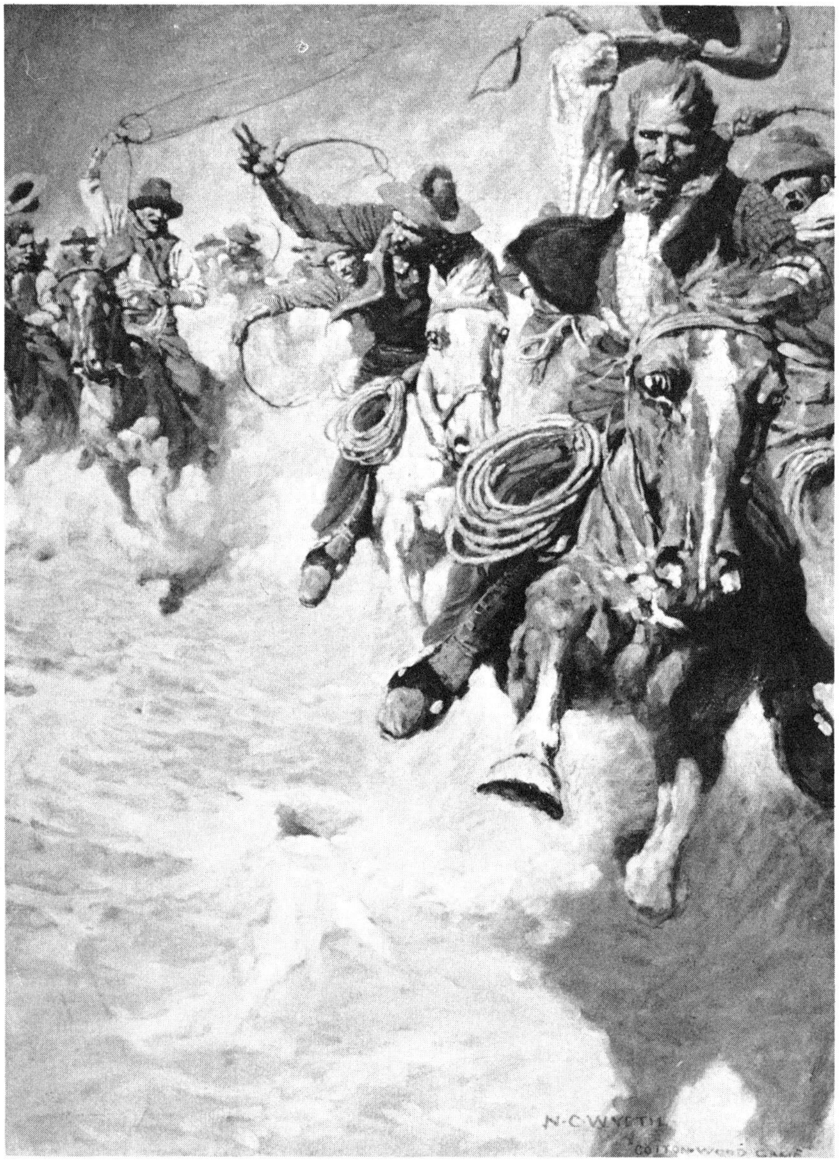

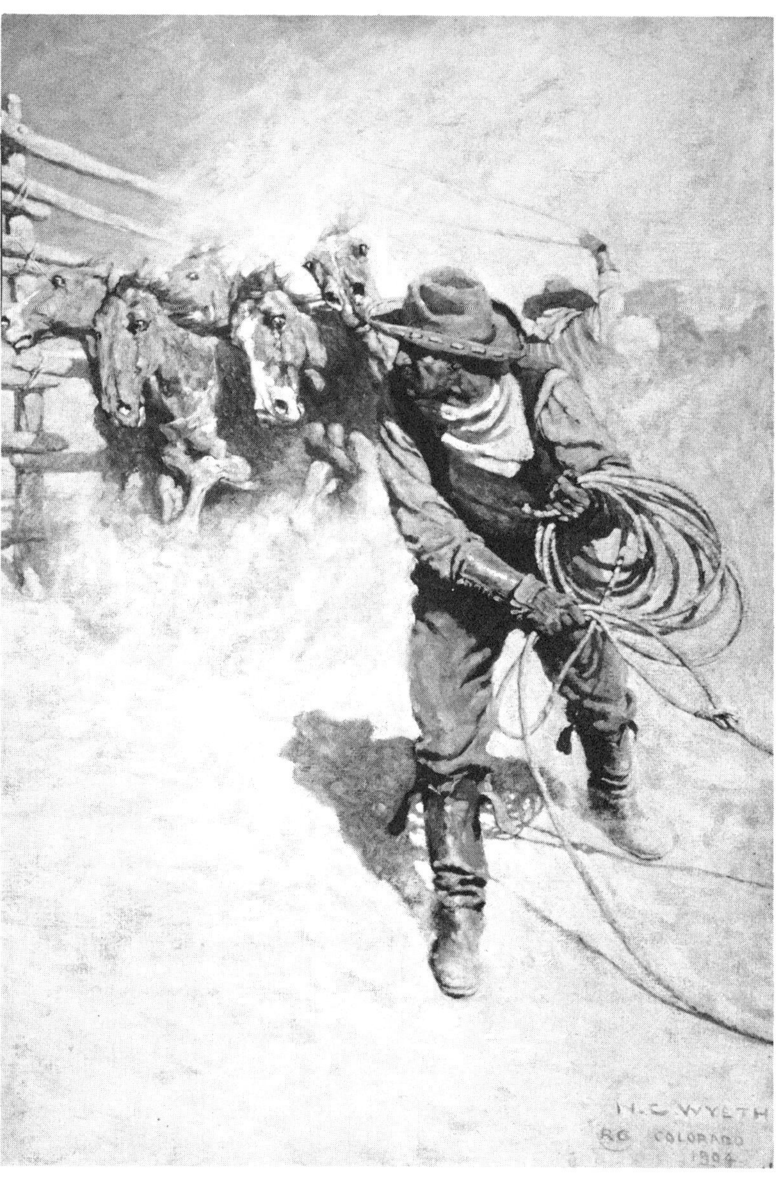

VAMOOSE, N. C. Wyeth, oil, 38"x26"
Lent by Mr. John M. Schiff

IN THE CORRAL, N. C. Wyeth, oil, 38"x26"
Lent by Mr. John M. Schiff

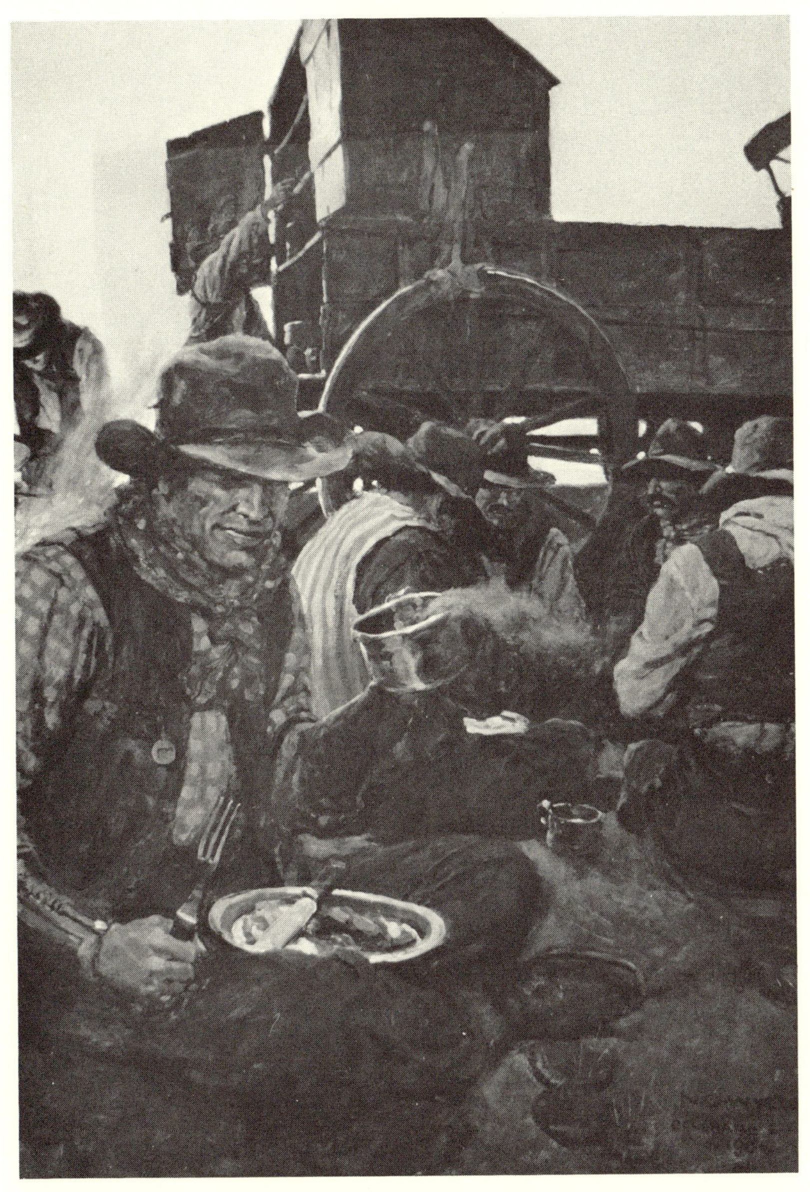

DINNER TIME, N. C. Wyeth, oil, 38"x26"
Lent by Mr. John M. Schiff

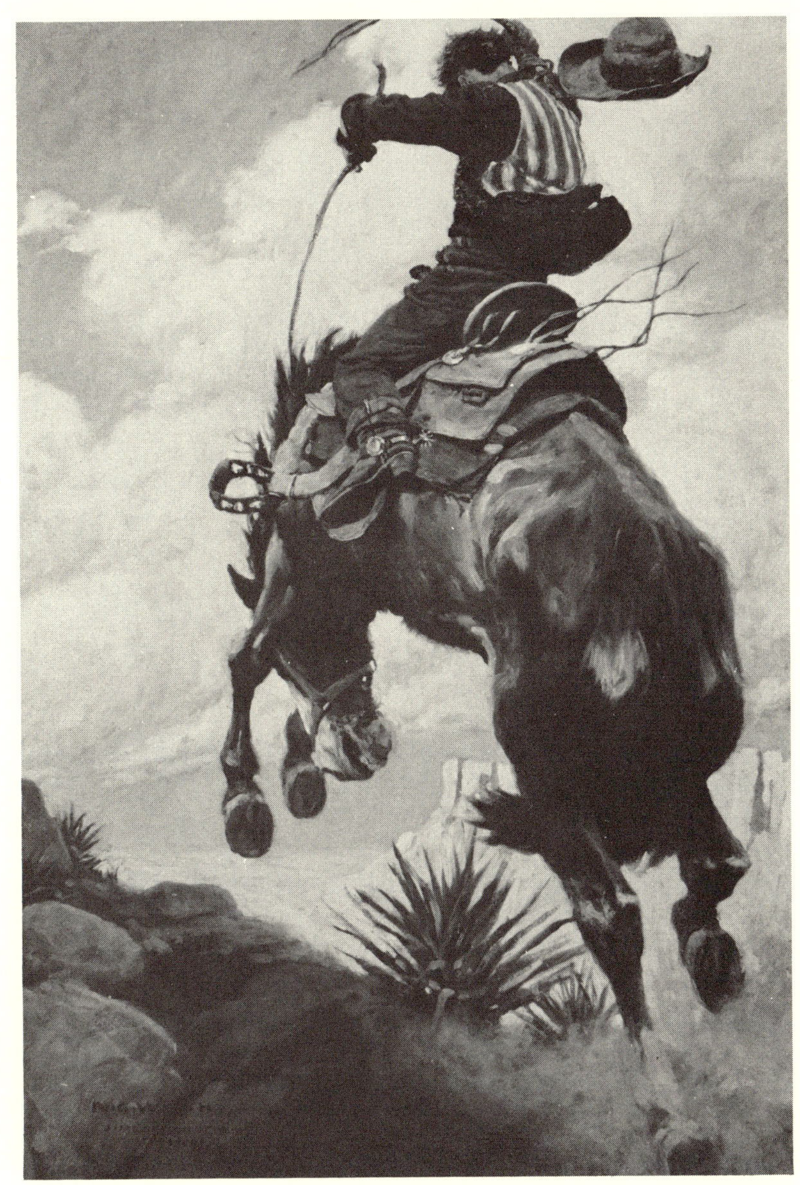

SUNFISHER, N. C. Wyeth, oil, 38"x26"
Lent by Mr. John M. Schiff

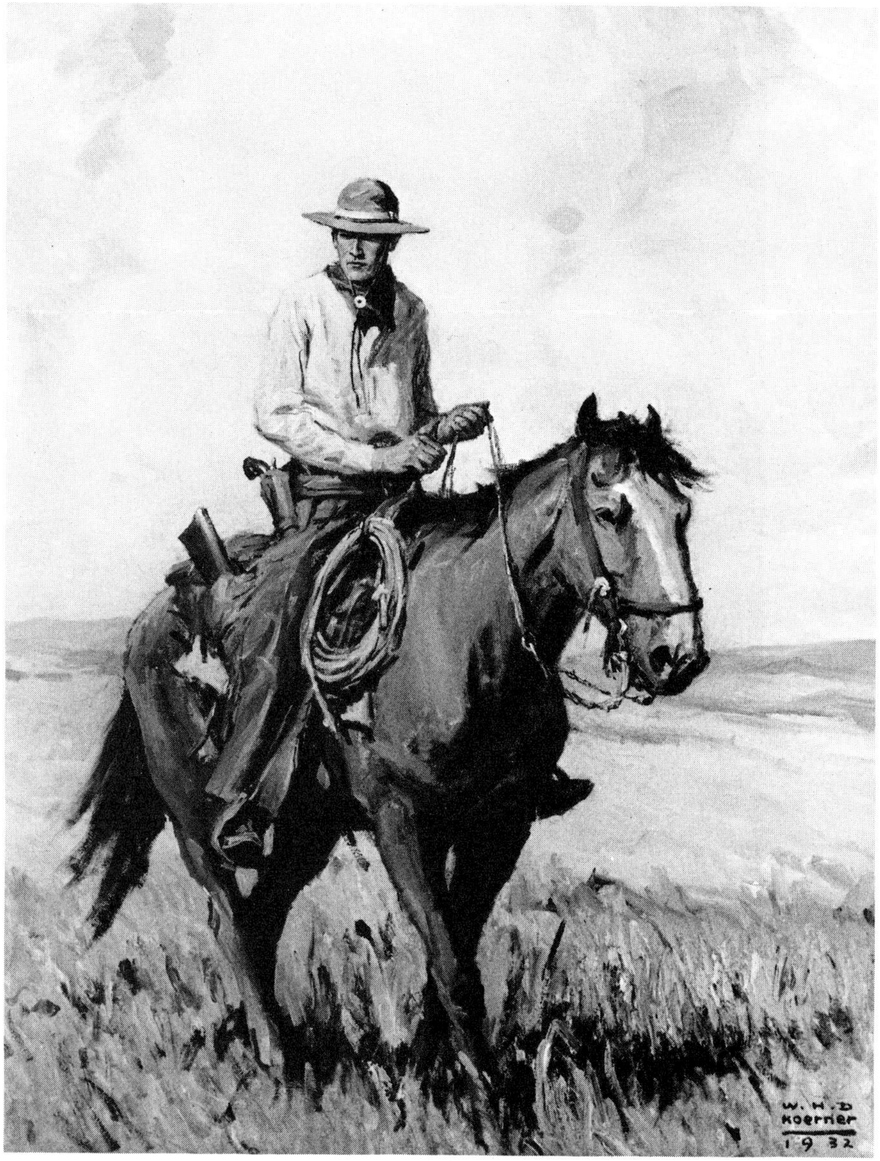

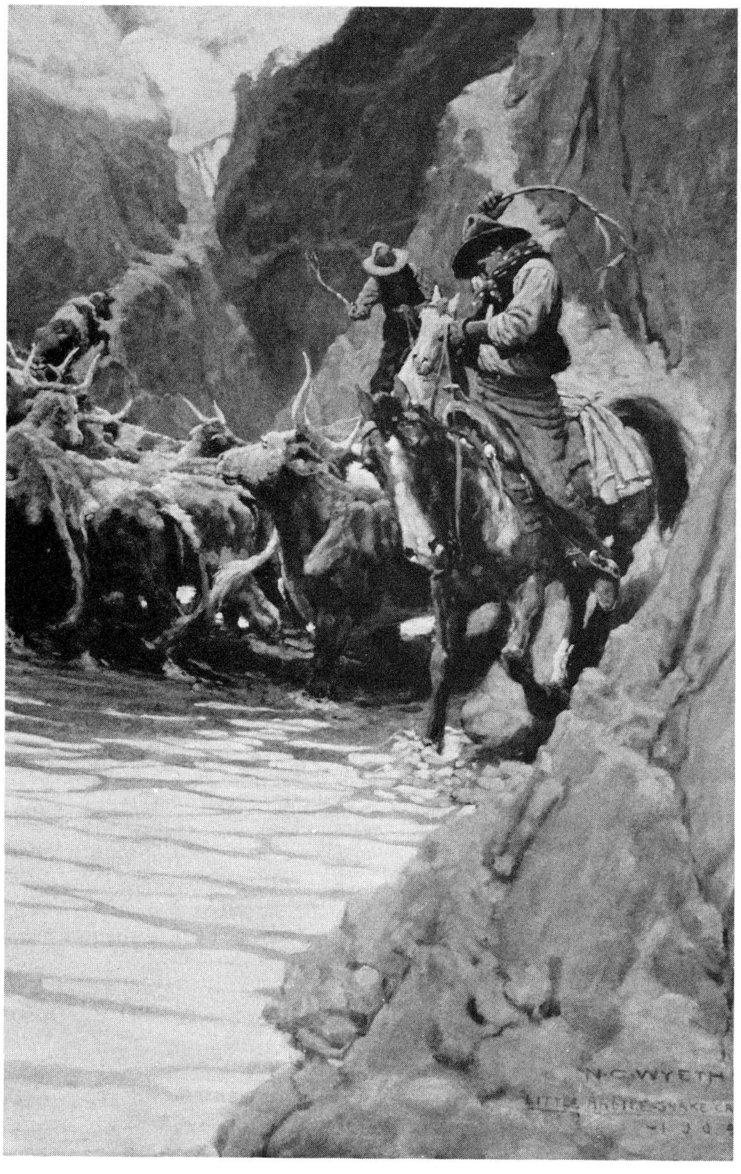

THROUGH SHORT GRASS COUNTRY, W. H. D. Koerner, oil, 28"x40"
Lent by the artist's daughter

UP THE CANYON, N. C. Wyeth, oil, 38"x26"
Lent by Mr. John M. Schiff

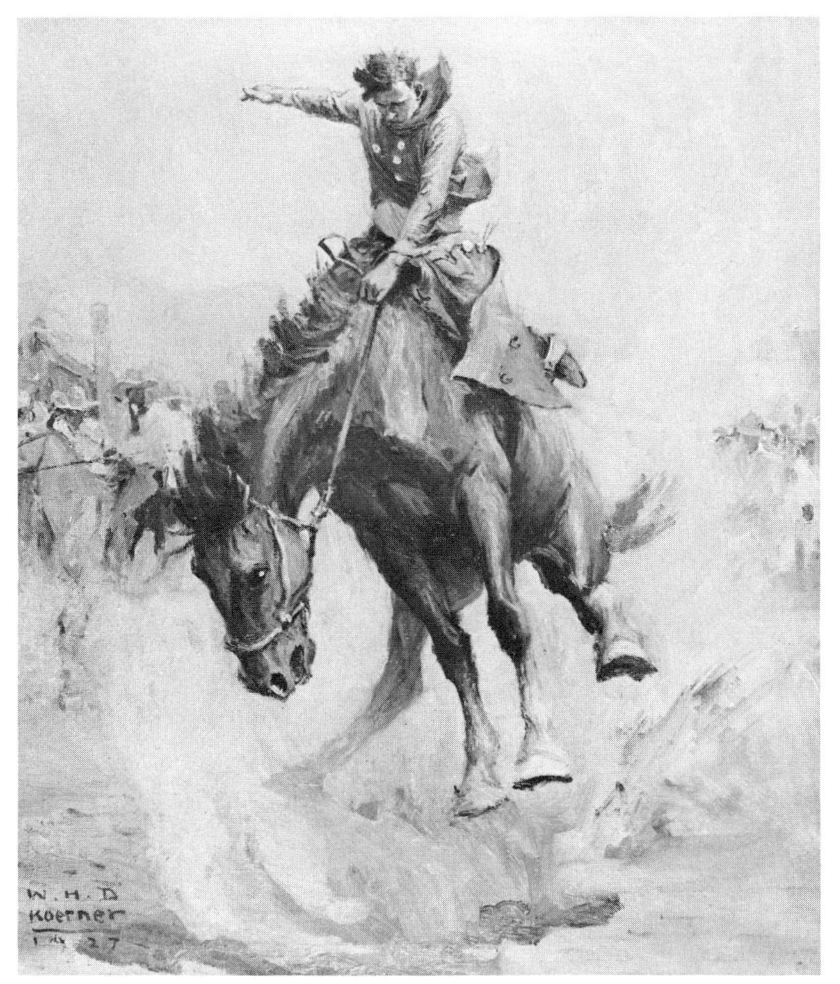

ROCK CRUSHER, W. H. D. Koerner, oil, 36"x30"
Lent by the artist's daughter

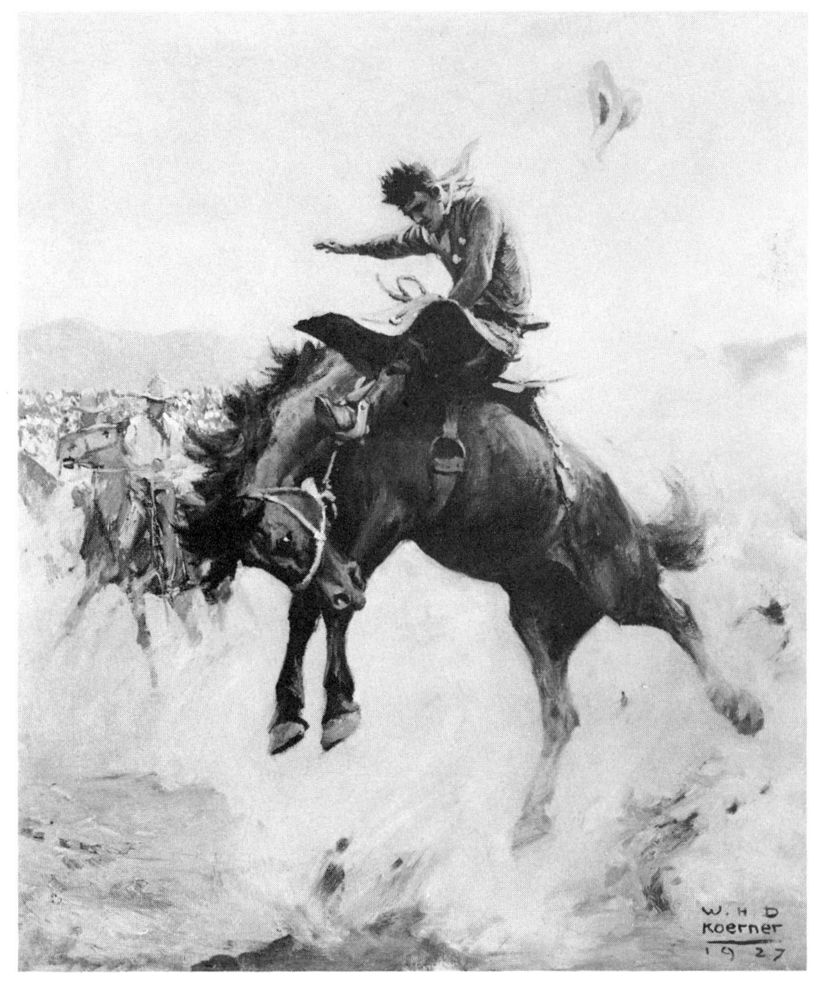

LOST ECSTACY, W. H. D. Koerner, oil, 36¼"x30"
Lent by Harrison Eiteljorg

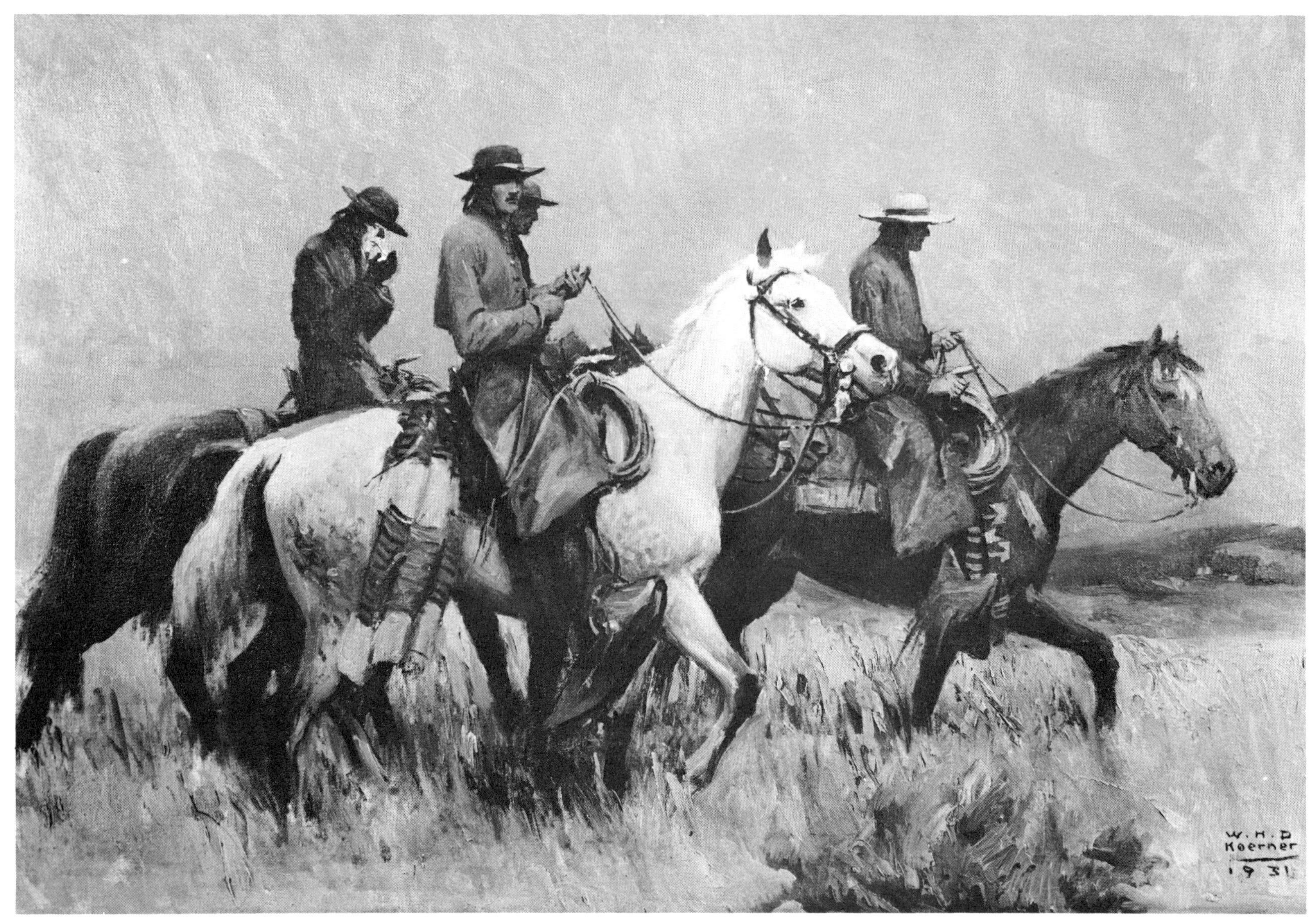

VAQUEROS, W. H. D. Koerner, oil, 28"x40"
Lent by the artist's daughter

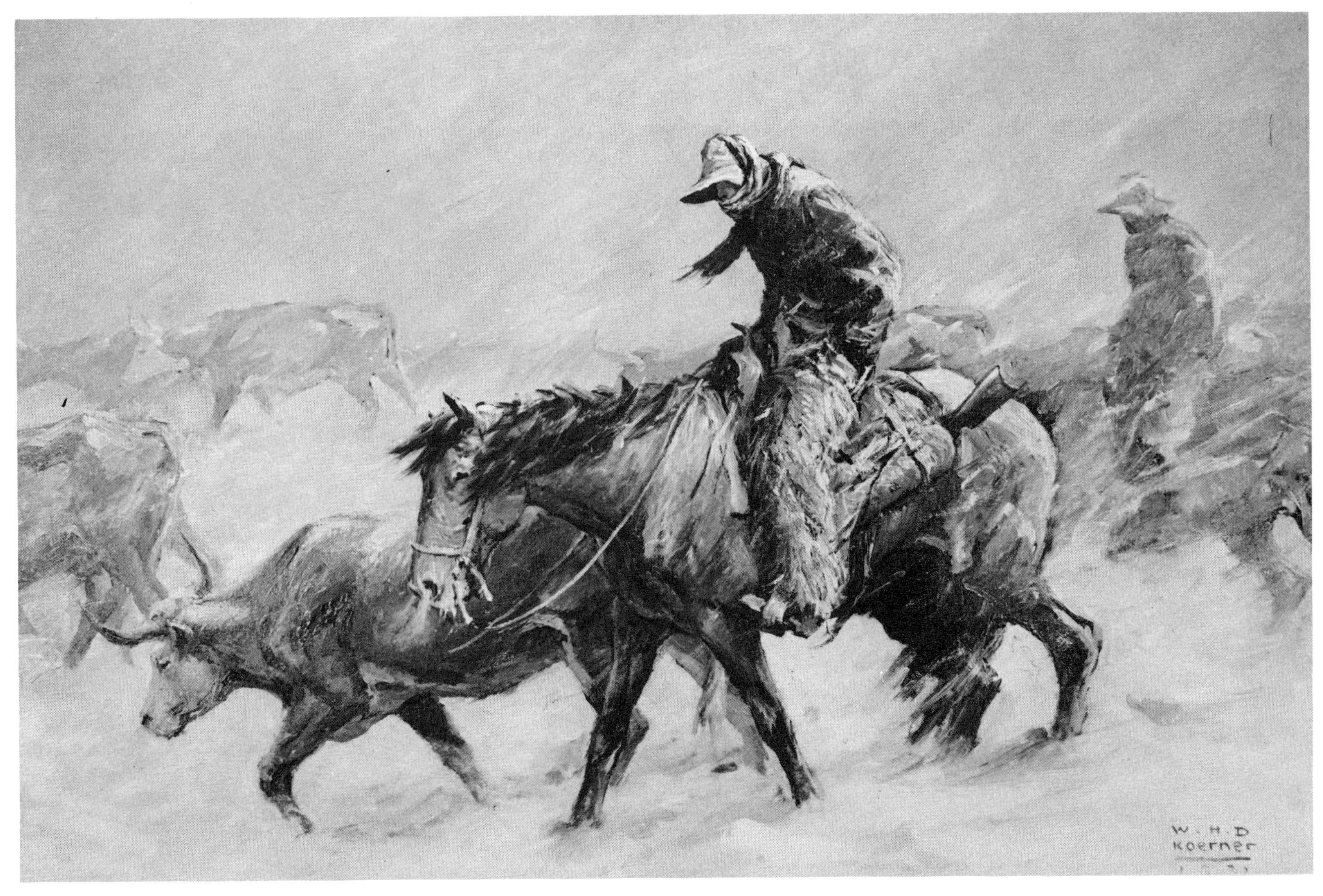

HARD WINTER, W. H. D. Koerner, oil, 28"x40"
Lent by the artist's daughter

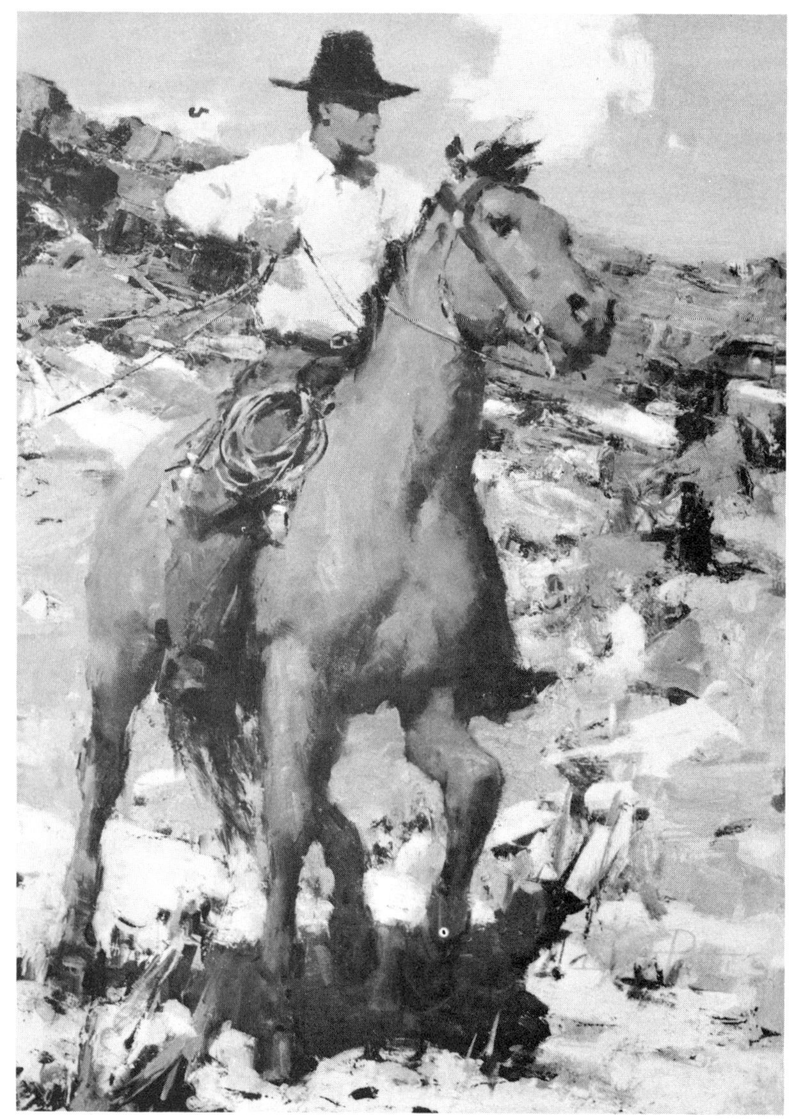

ROUGH GOING, Burt Proctor, oil, 30"x24"
Lent by Eugene B. Adkins

BRANDING - 1968, James Bama, oil, 30"x24"
Lent by Mrs. Helen Gleim

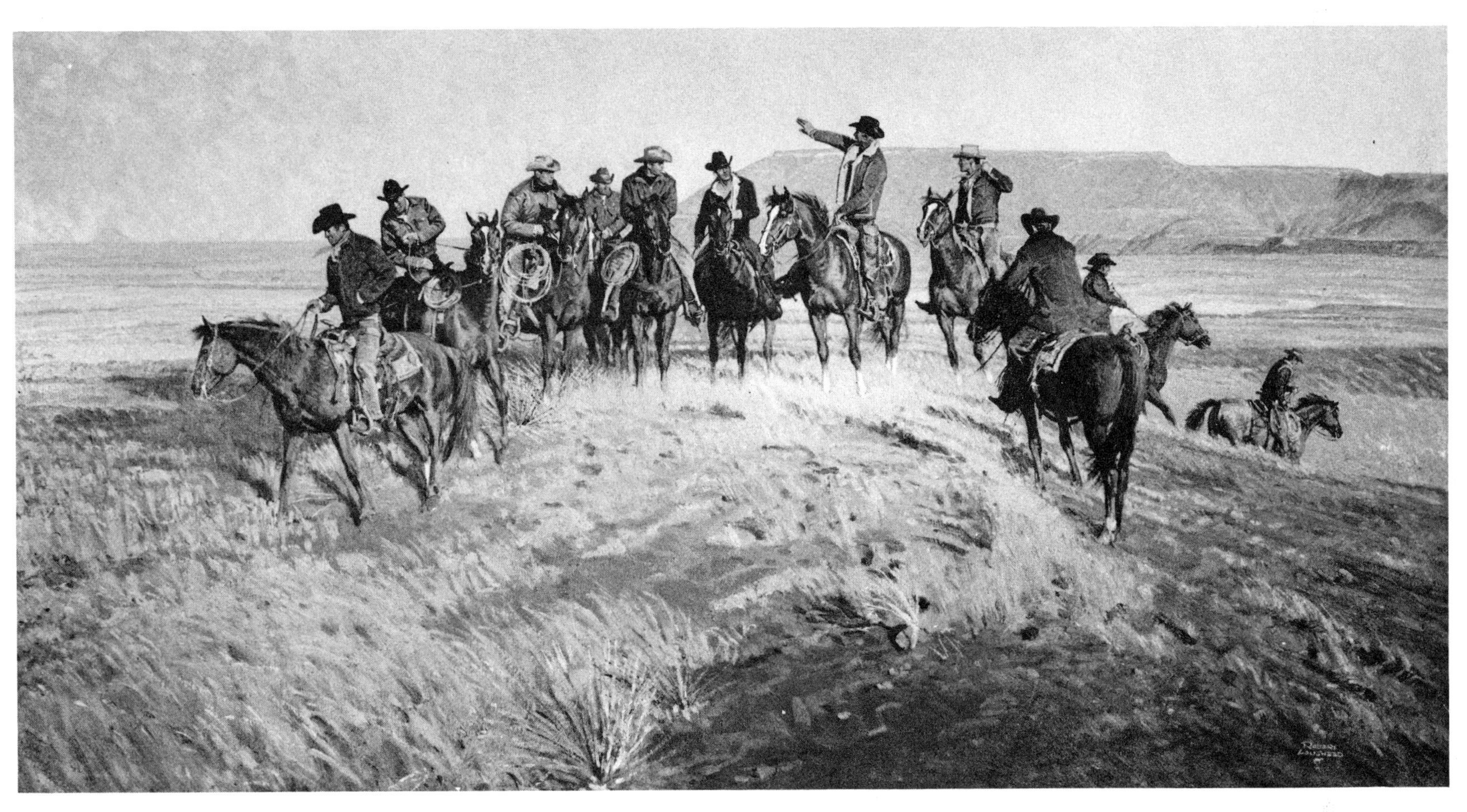

SCATTERING THE BELL RIDERS, Robert Lougheed, oil, 36"x66"
Lent by Mr. and Mrs. Robert K. Hillin

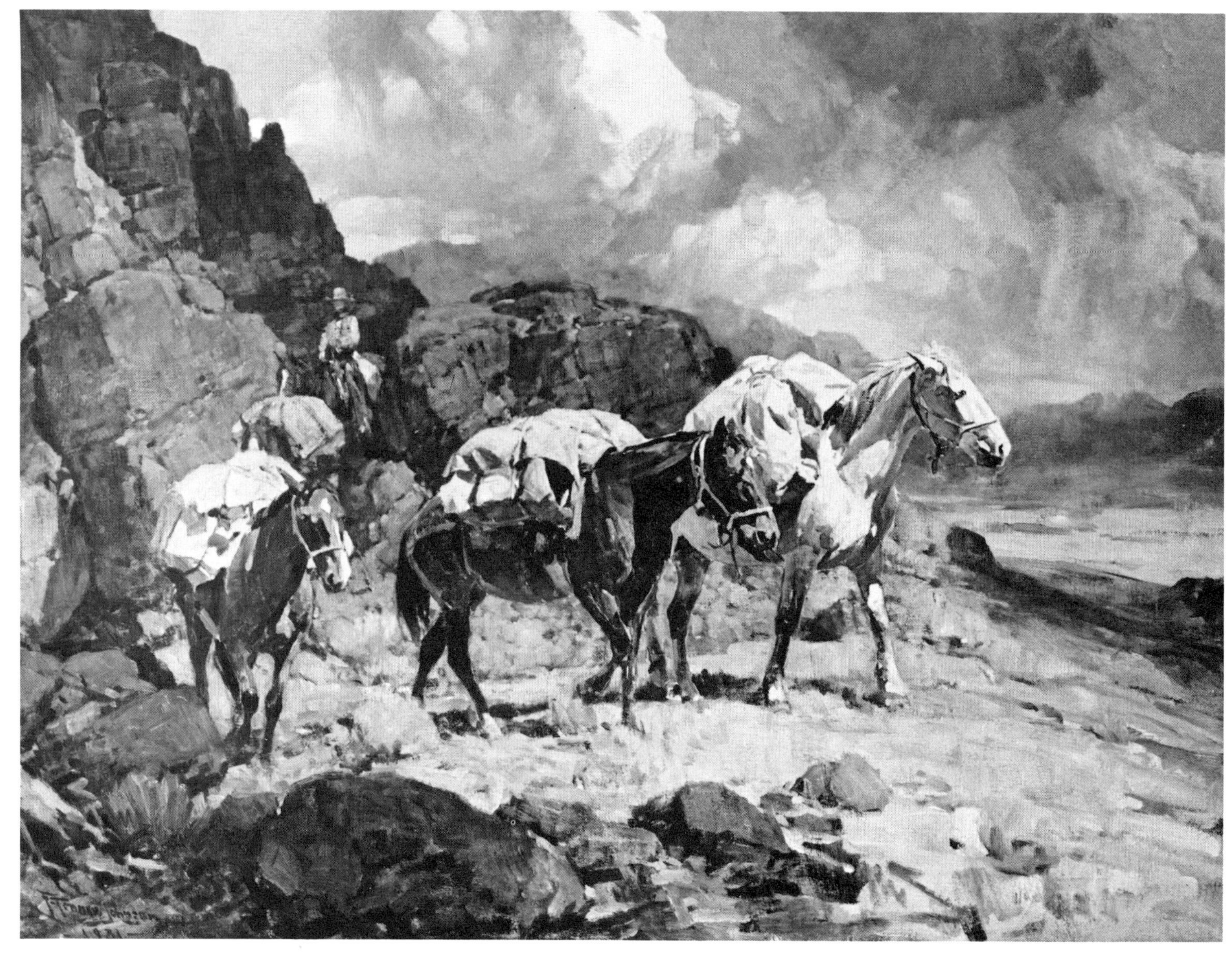

PACK HORSES OUT OF RIMROCK RANCH, Frank Tenney Johnson, 36"x46"
Lent by Eugene B. Adkins

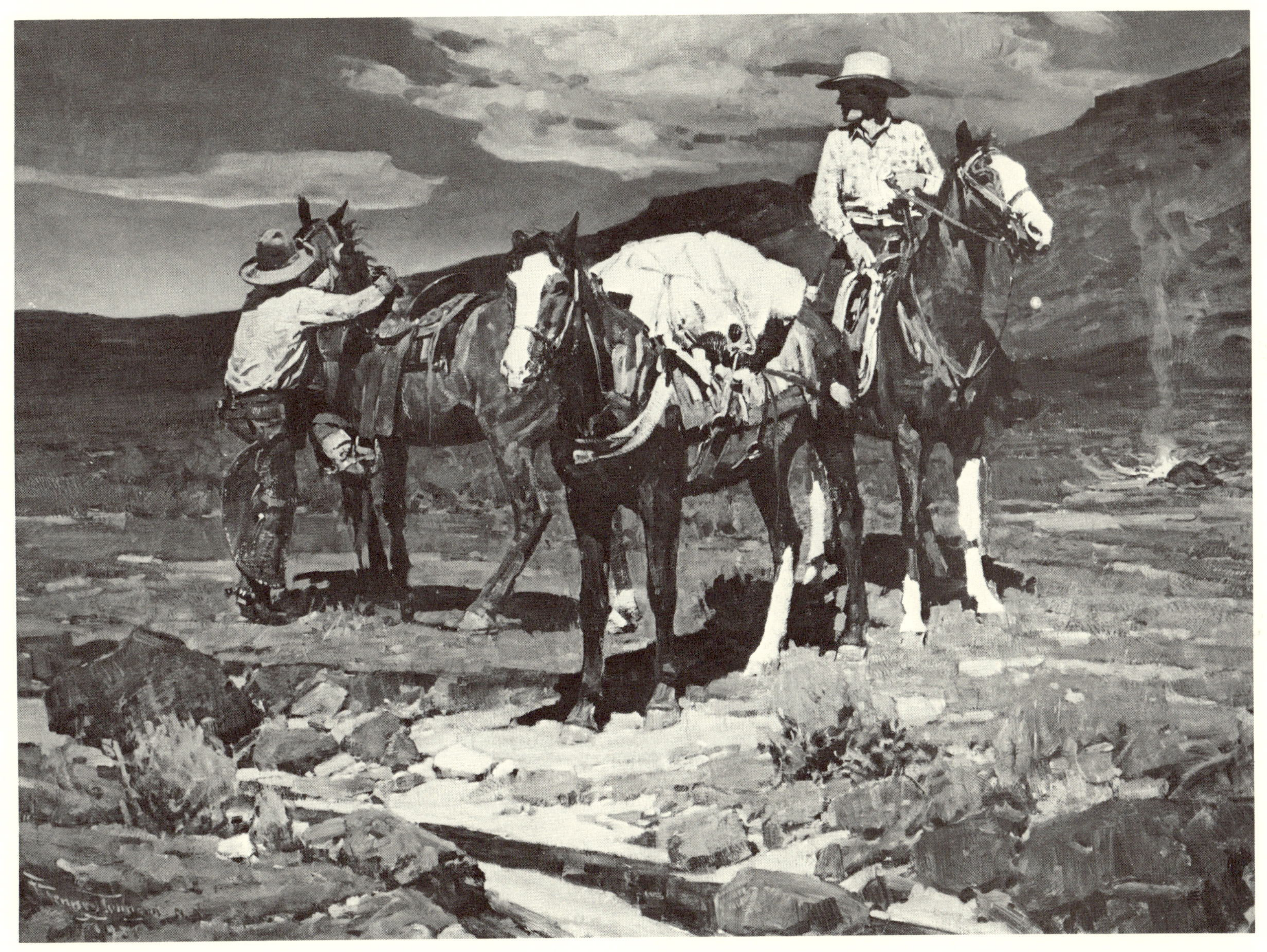

AT THE FIRST STREAK OF DAWN, Frank Tenney Johnson, 28"x36"
Lent by Mr. and Mrs. Charles W. Duncan, Jr.

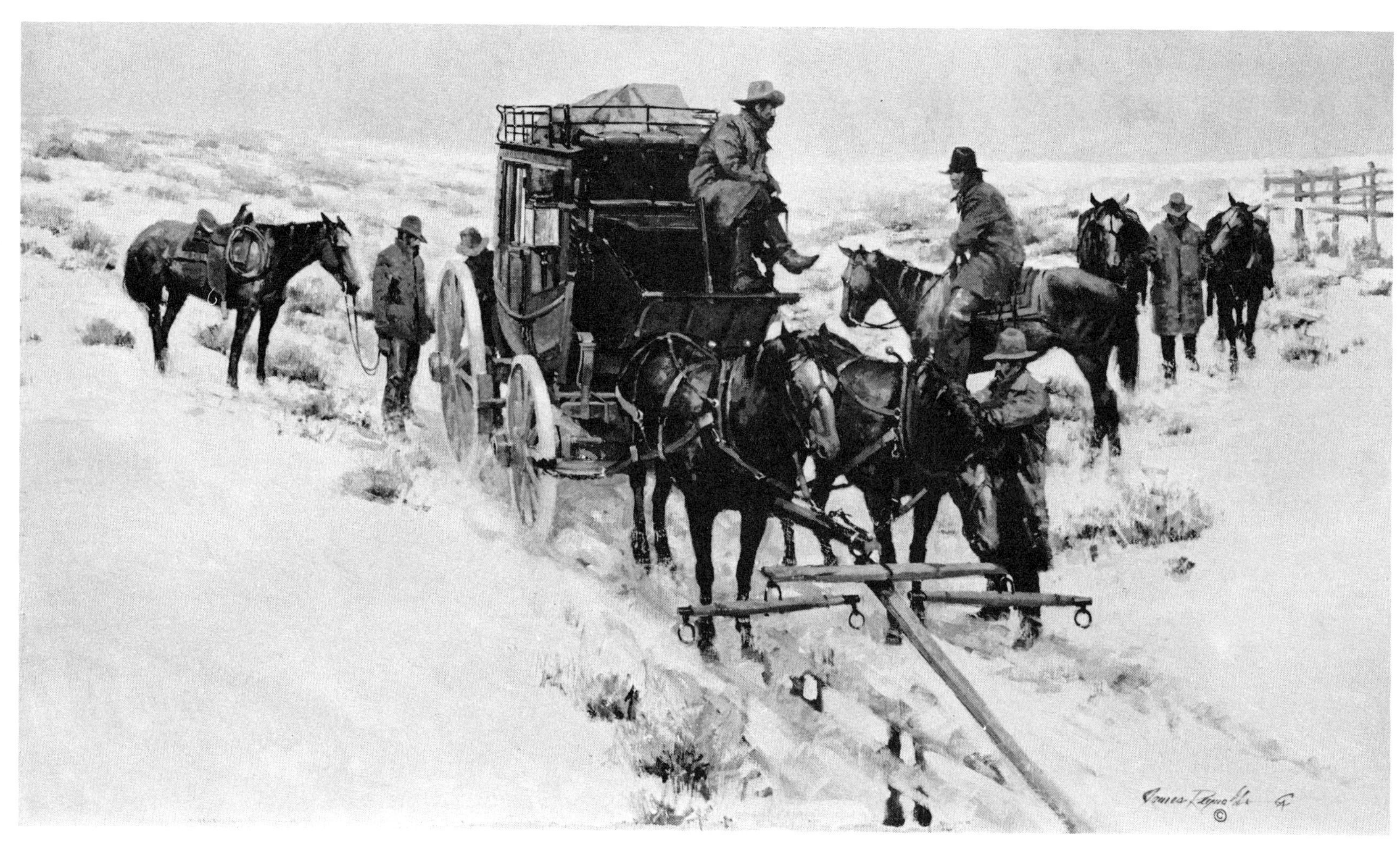

STAGE STOP, James E. Reynolds, oil, 28"x48"
Lent by Harrison Eiteljorg

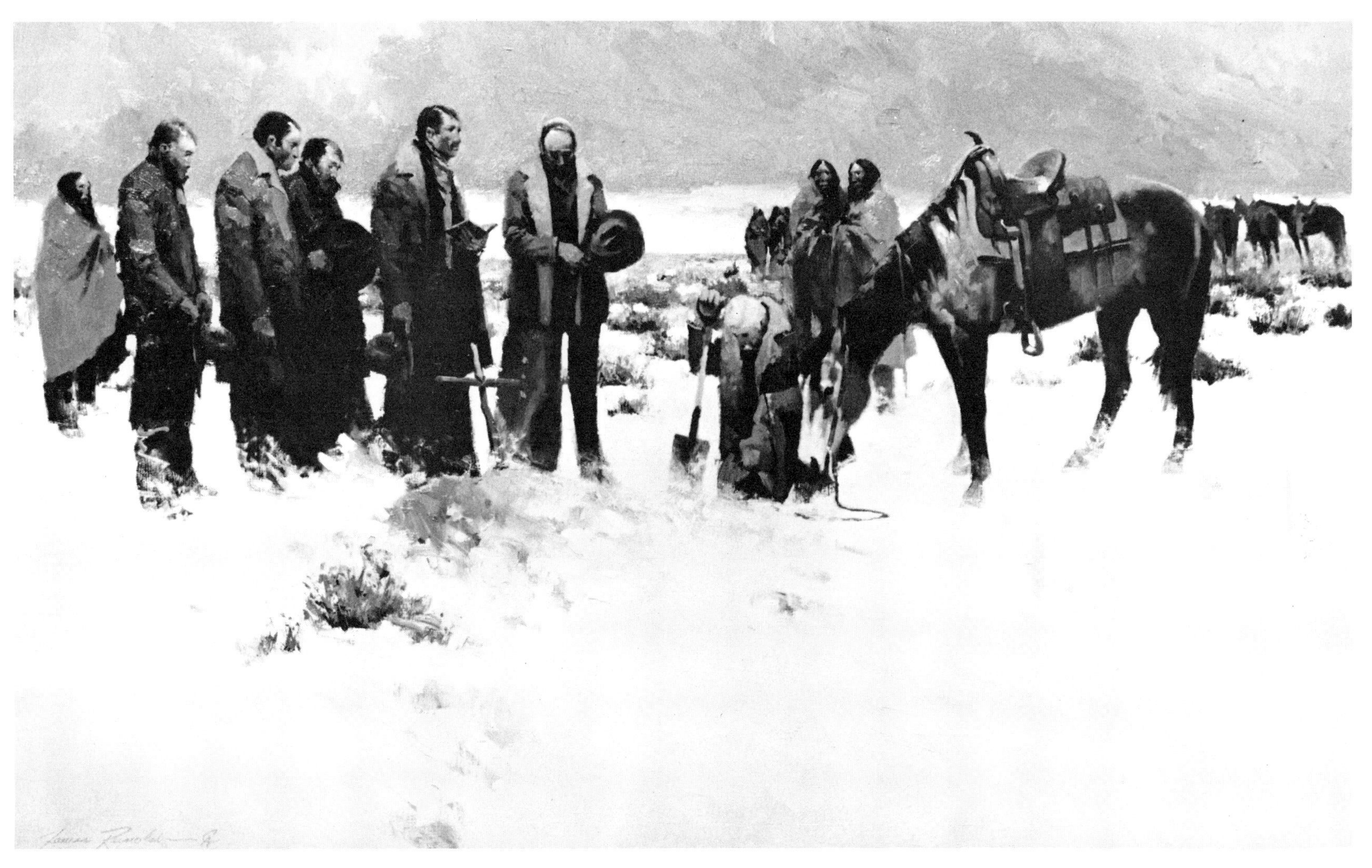

THE LORD IS MY SHEPHERD, James E. Reynolds, oil, 27"x43¼"
Lent by Phoenix Art Museum, Phoenix, Arizona

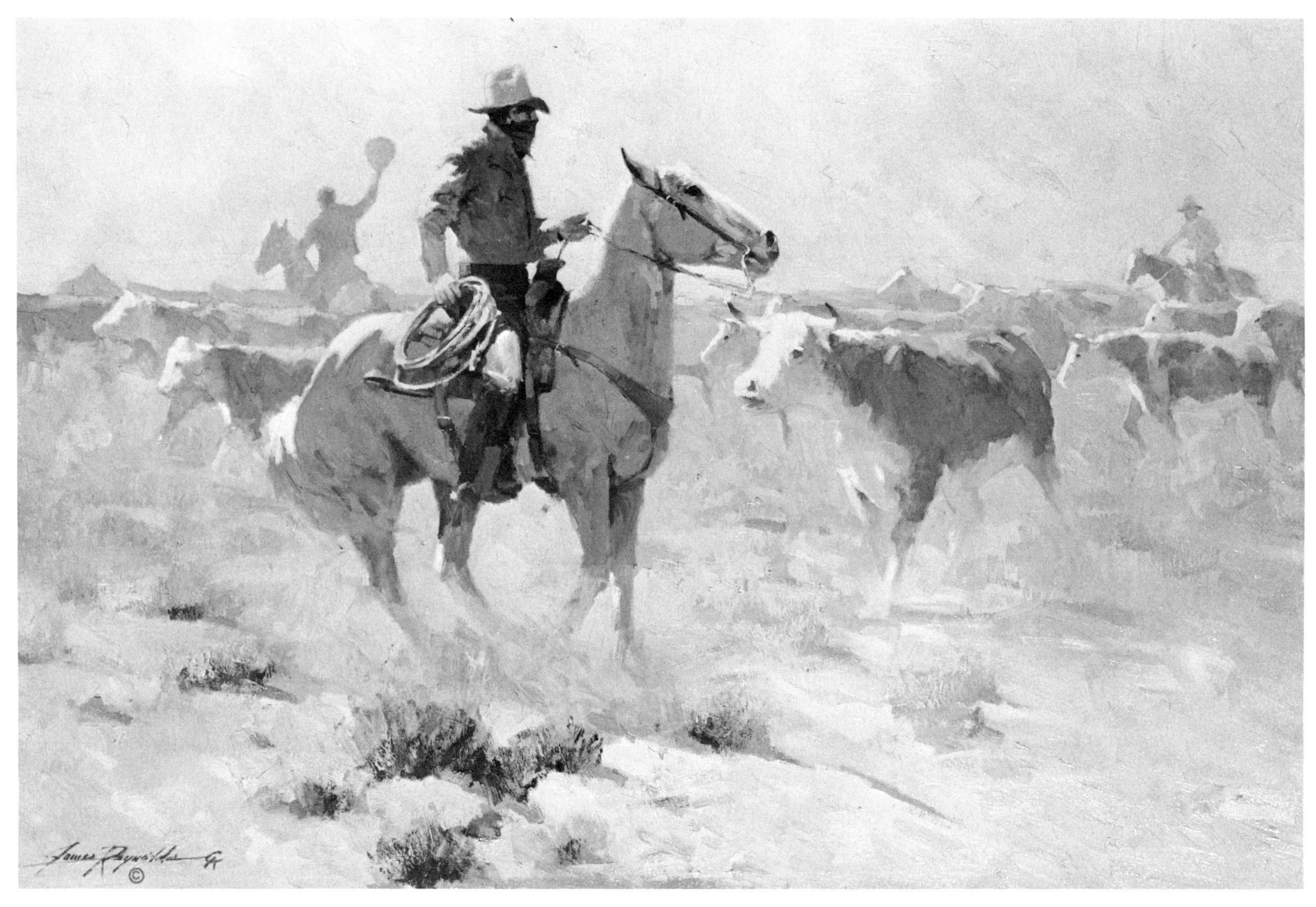

NOWHERE TO GO, James E. Reynolds, oil, 24"x36"
Lent by Harrison Eiteljorg

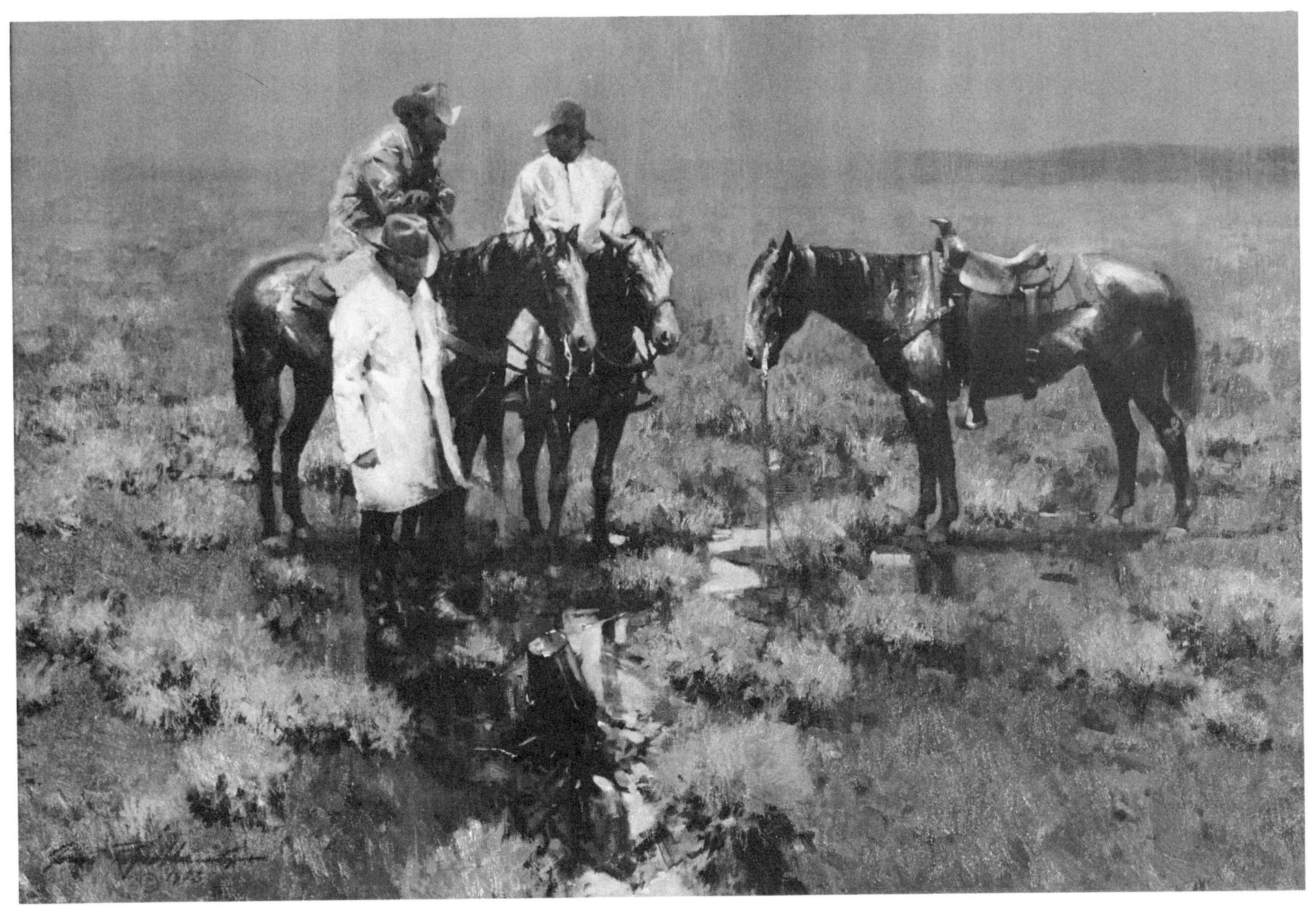

COLD COFFEE, James E. Reynolds, oil, 28"x48"
Lent by Mr. and Mrs. Robert K. Hillin

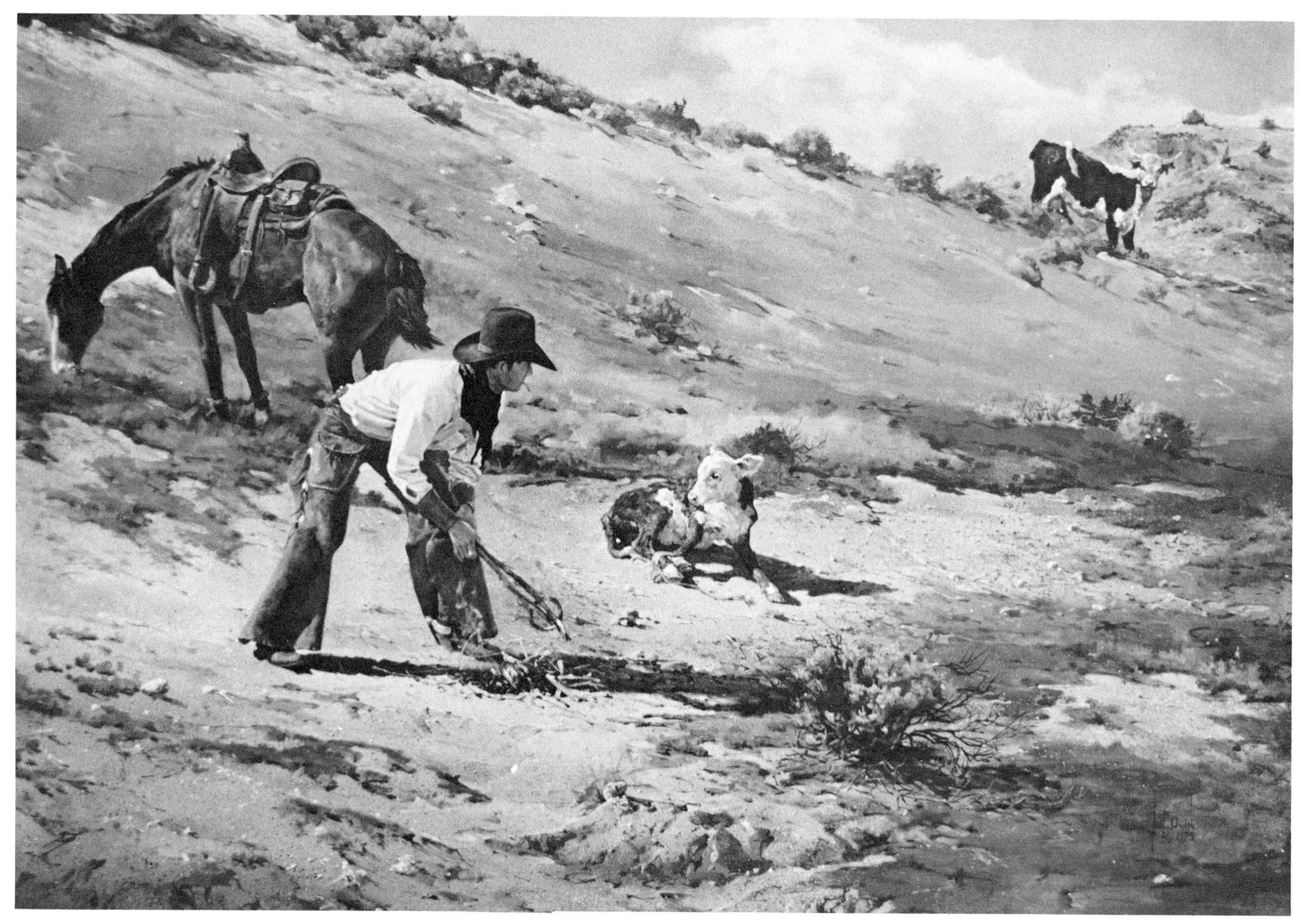

ONE EYE ON MOTHER, Bill Owen, oil, 30"x40"
Lent Anonymously

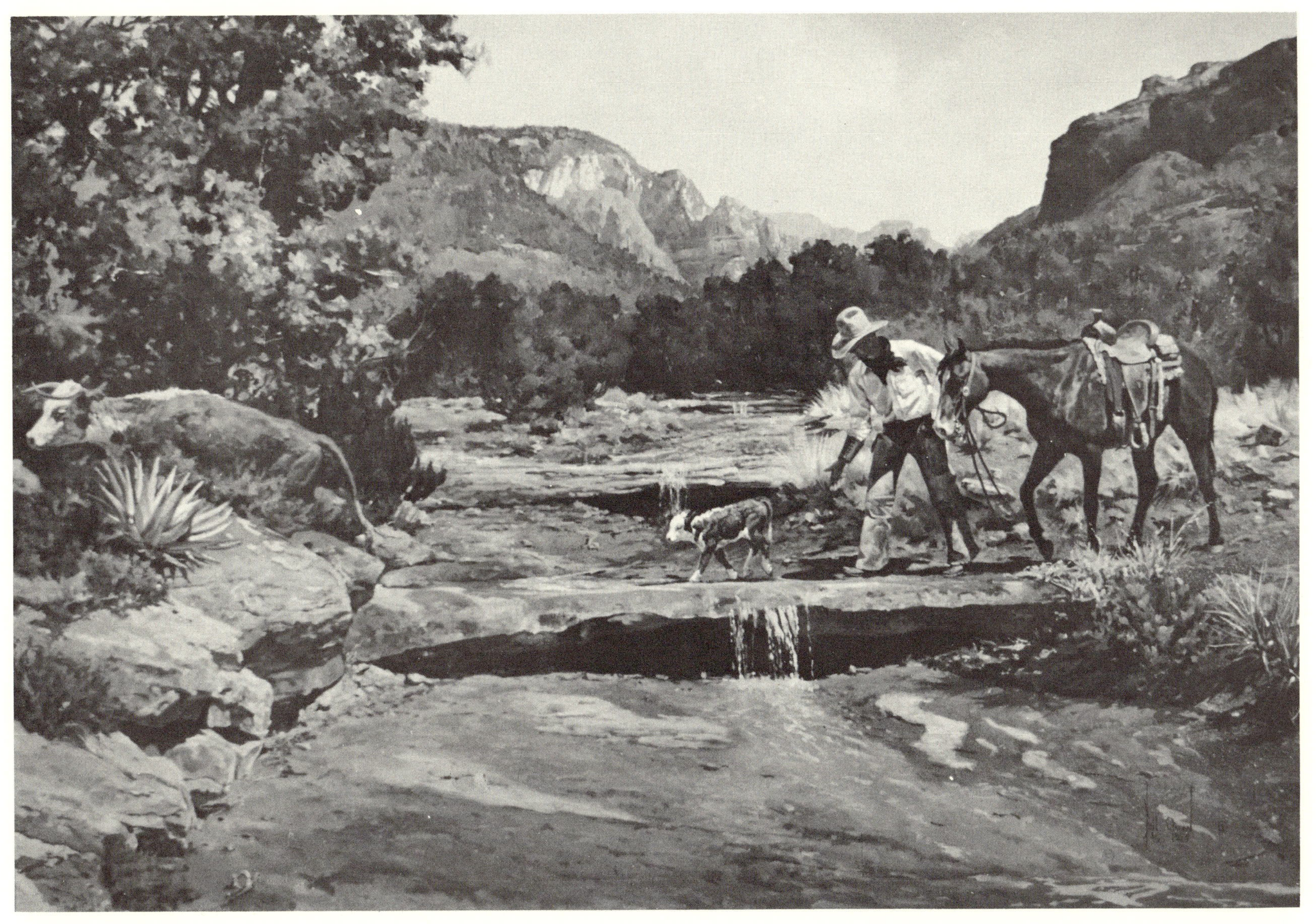

THE HELPING HAND, Bill Owen, oil, 30"x40"
Lent by Mr. and Mrs. Robert Rufenacht

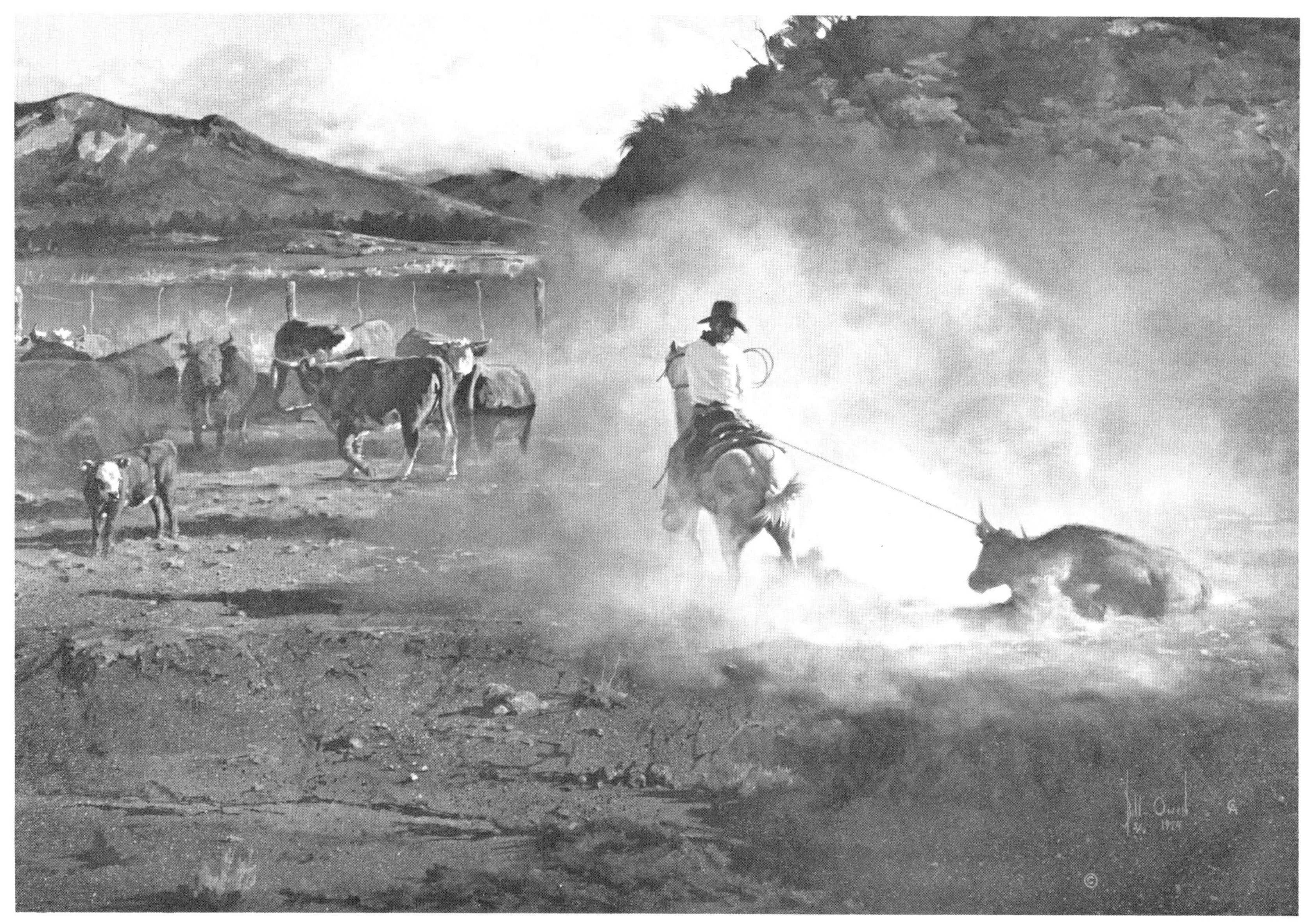

SULLED, Bill Owen, oil, 24"x36"
Lent by Tom and Betty Donato

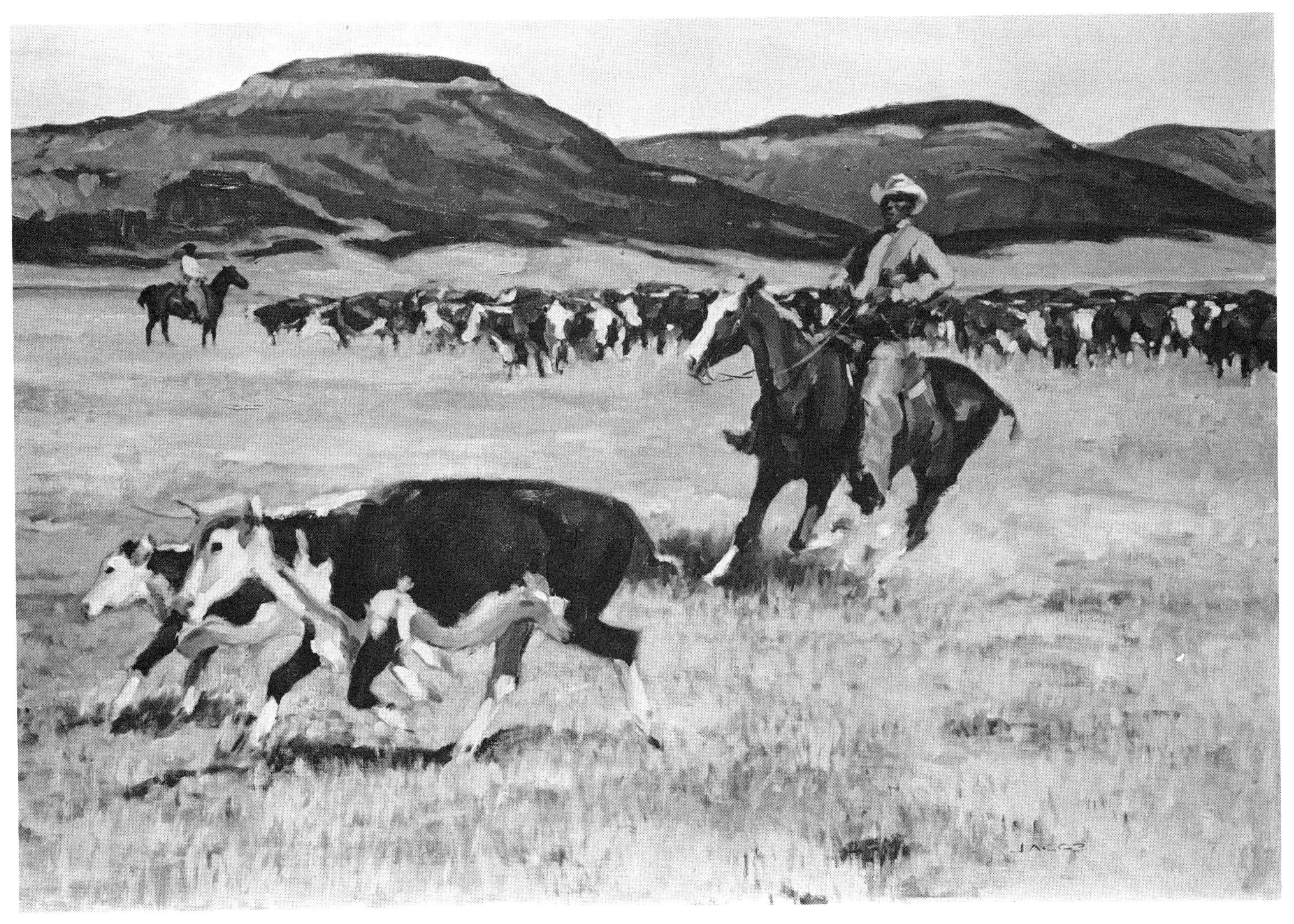

NEW MEXICO RANCH SCENE, Ned Jacob, oil, 24⅛"x36"
Lent by Harrison Eiteljorg

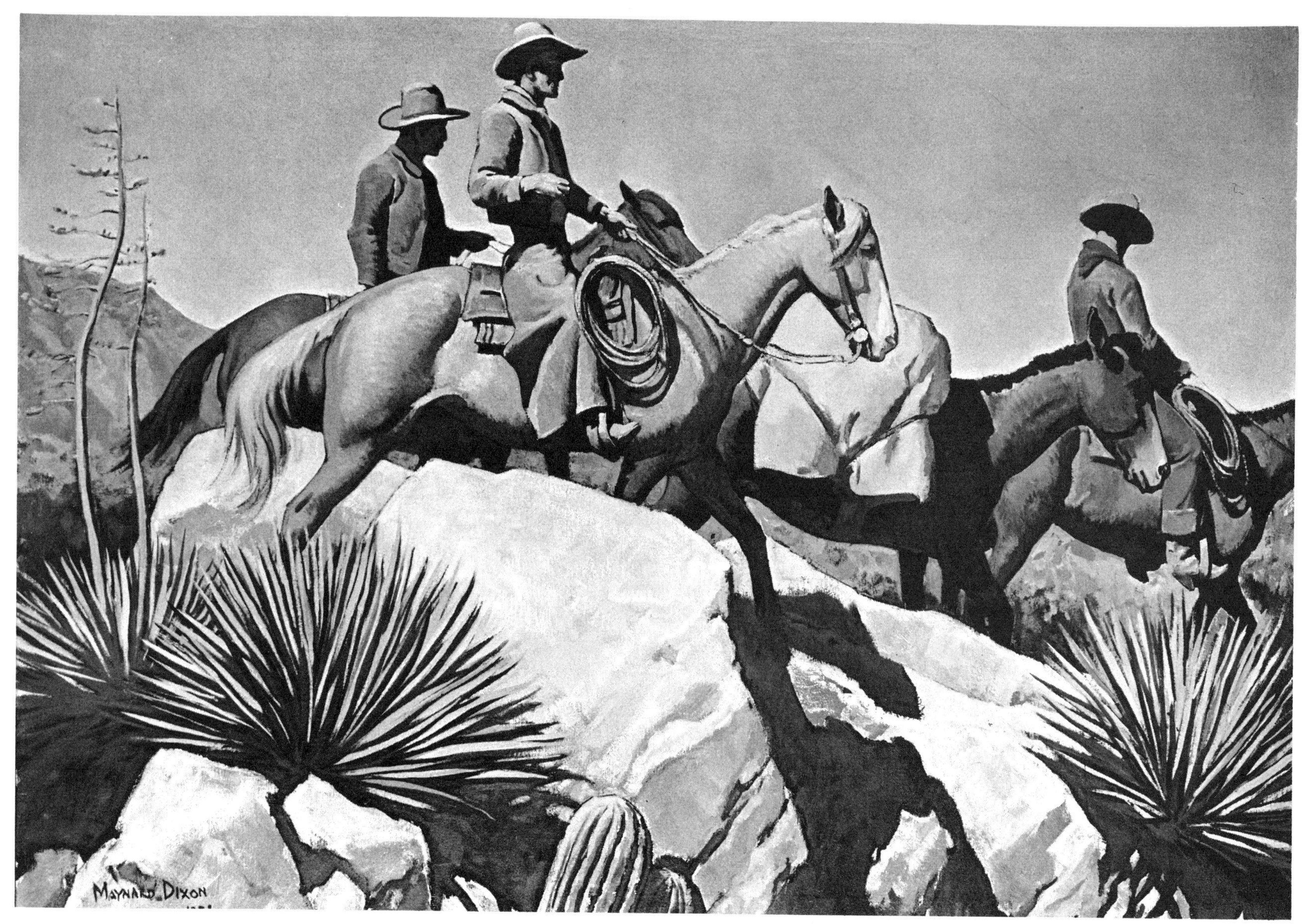

NO TRAIL, Maynard Dixon, oil, 30"x40"
Lent by Harrison Eiteljorg

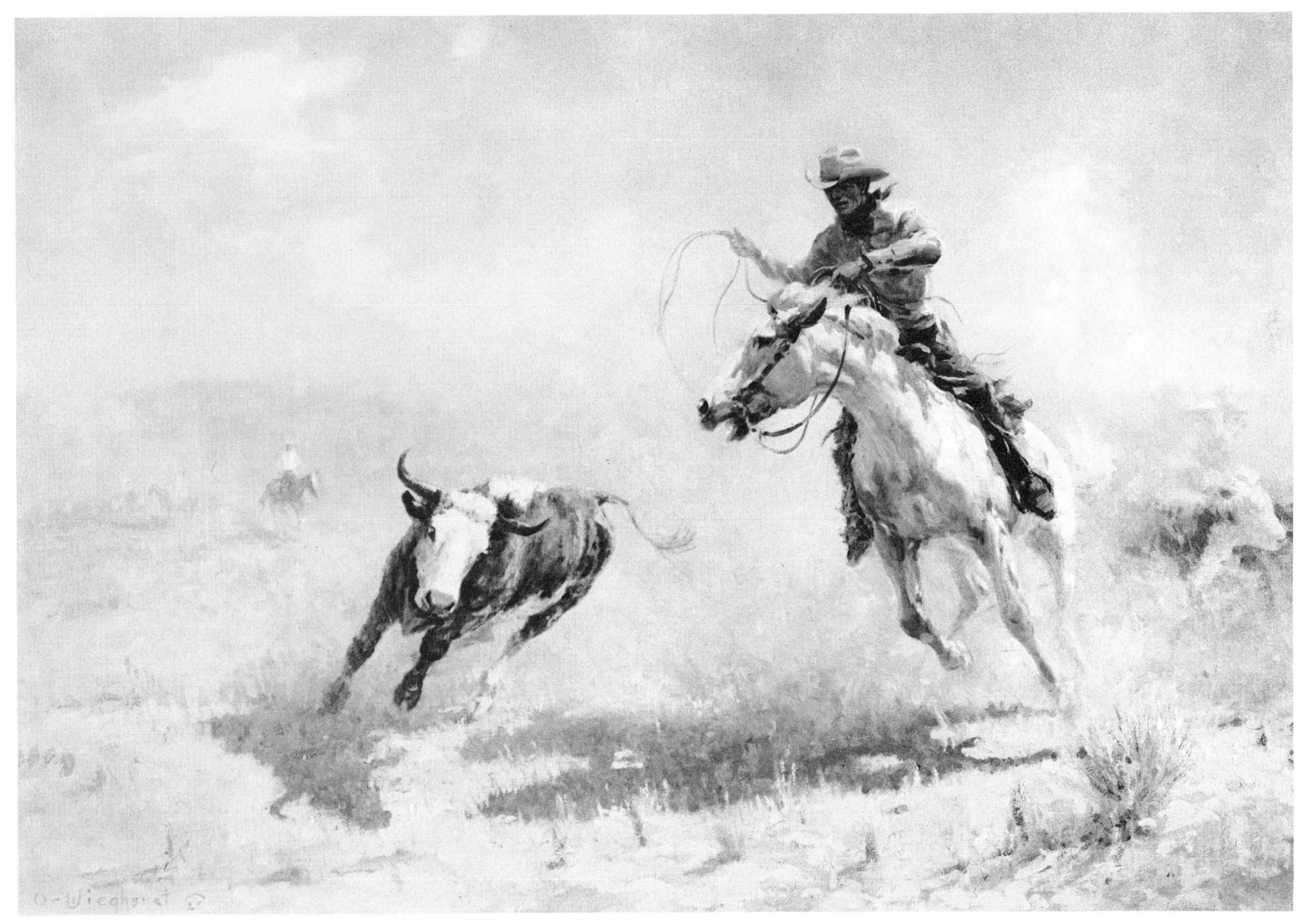

THE ROPER, Olaf Wieghorst, oil, 28⅛"x38"
Lent by Harrison Eiteljorg

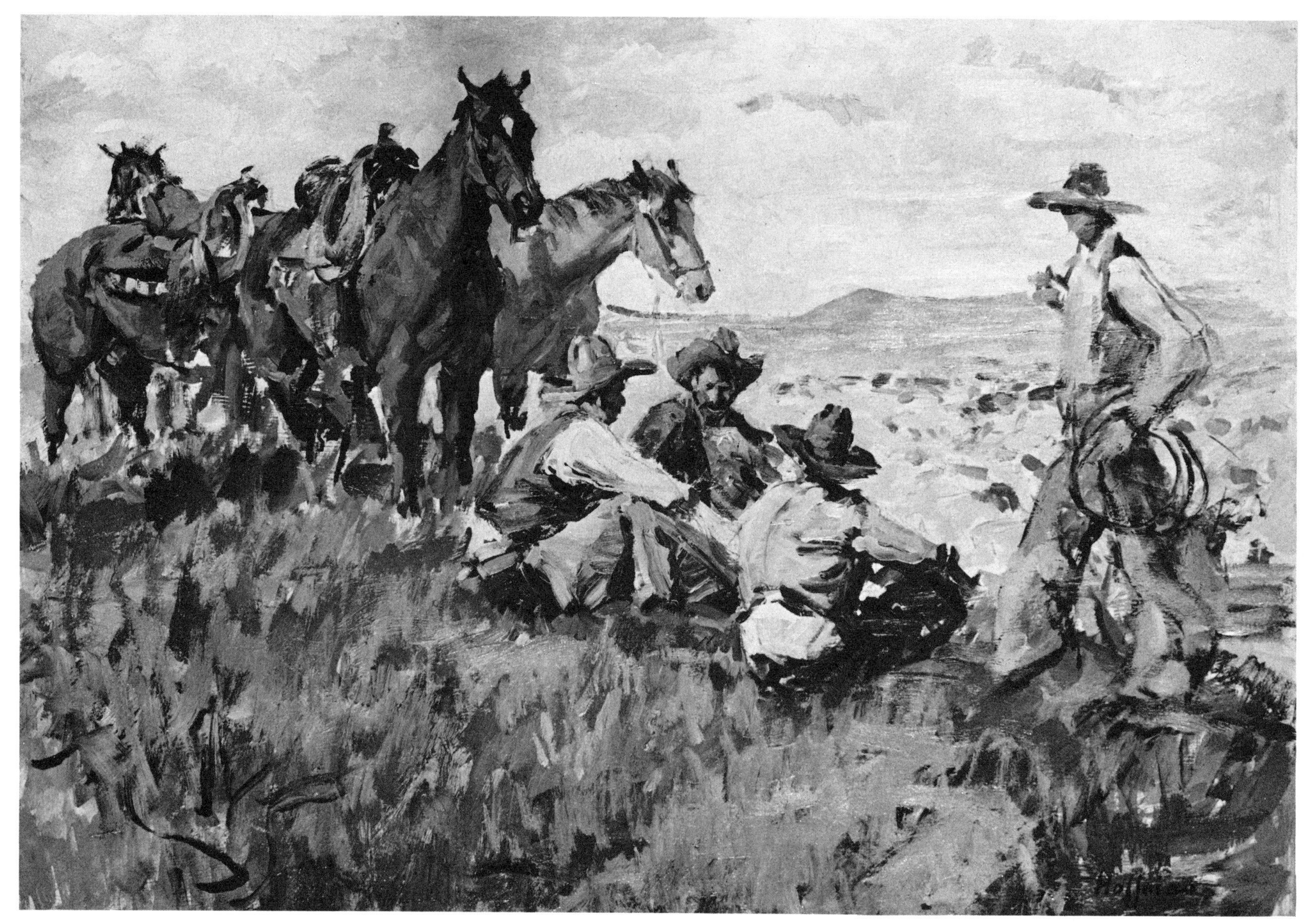

RESTING COWBOYS, Frank Hoffman, oil, 24"x31"
Lent by Harrison Eiteljorg

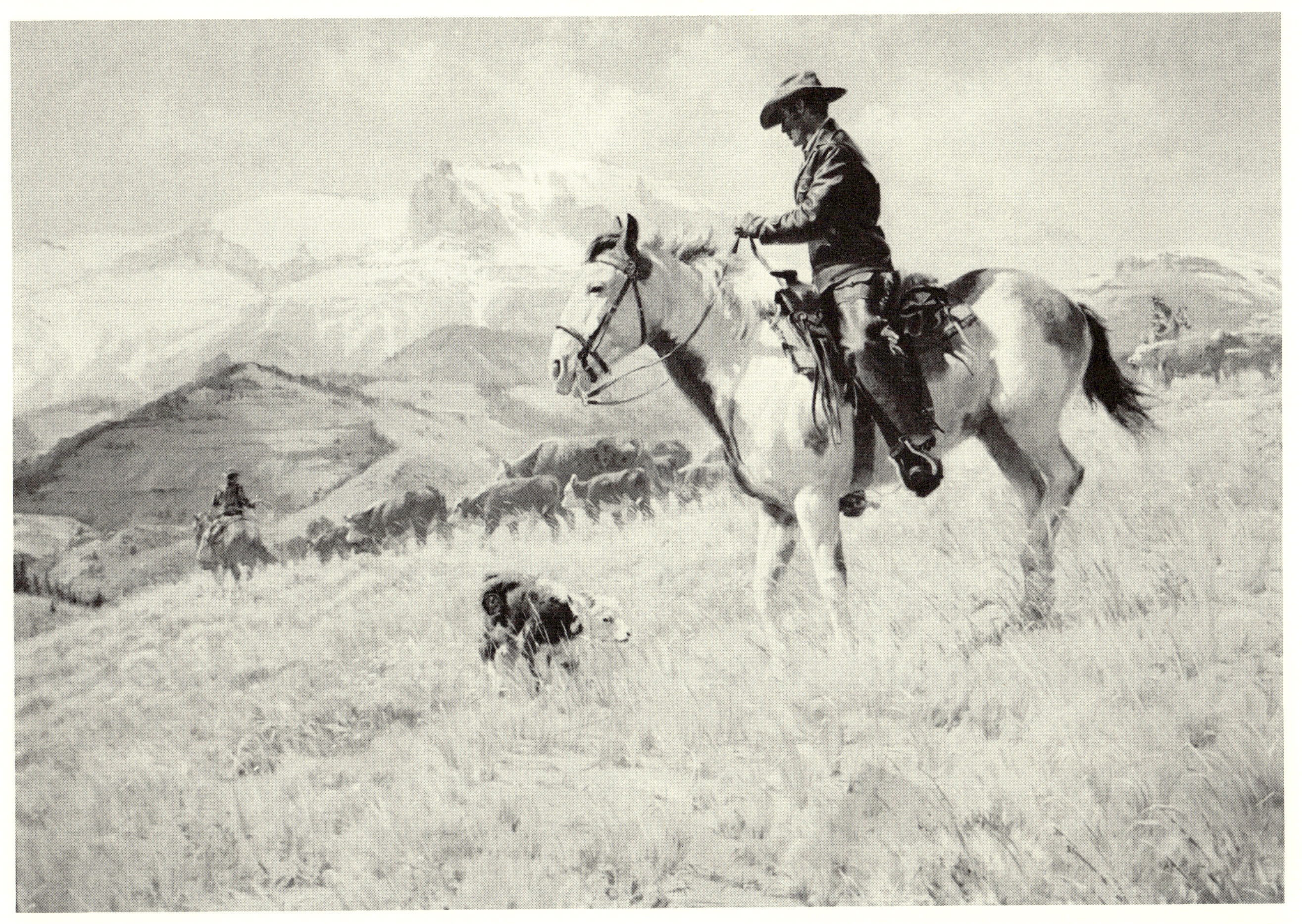

THE LITTLEST REBEL, Bob Meyers, oil, 24"x30"
Lent by Mr. and Mrs. H. P. Skoglund

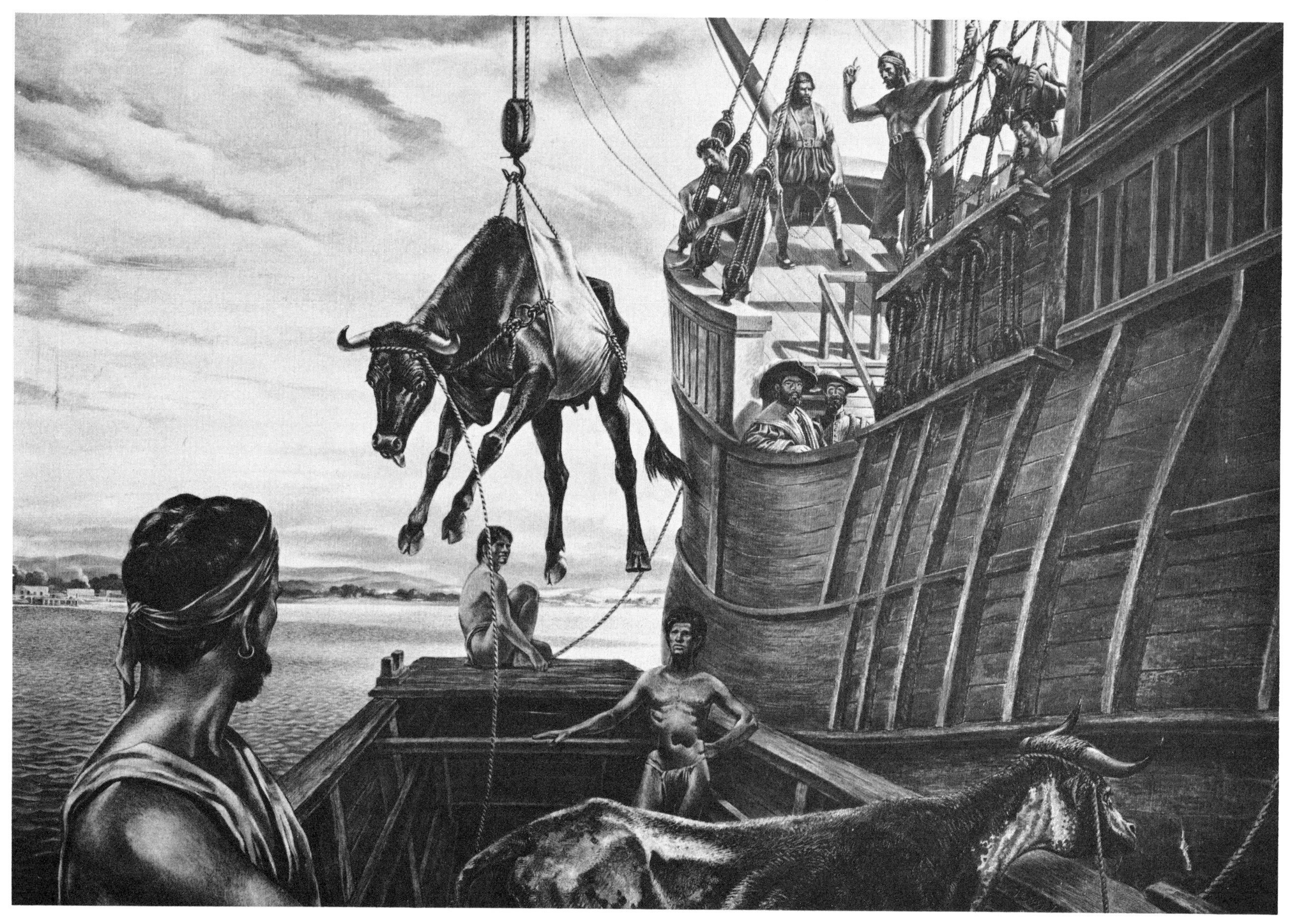

UNLOADING THE FIRST CATTLE IN NORTH AMERICA, VERA CRUZ, 1521, Tom Lea, oil, 22"x28"
Lent by Dallas Museum of Fine Arts, Dallas, Texas

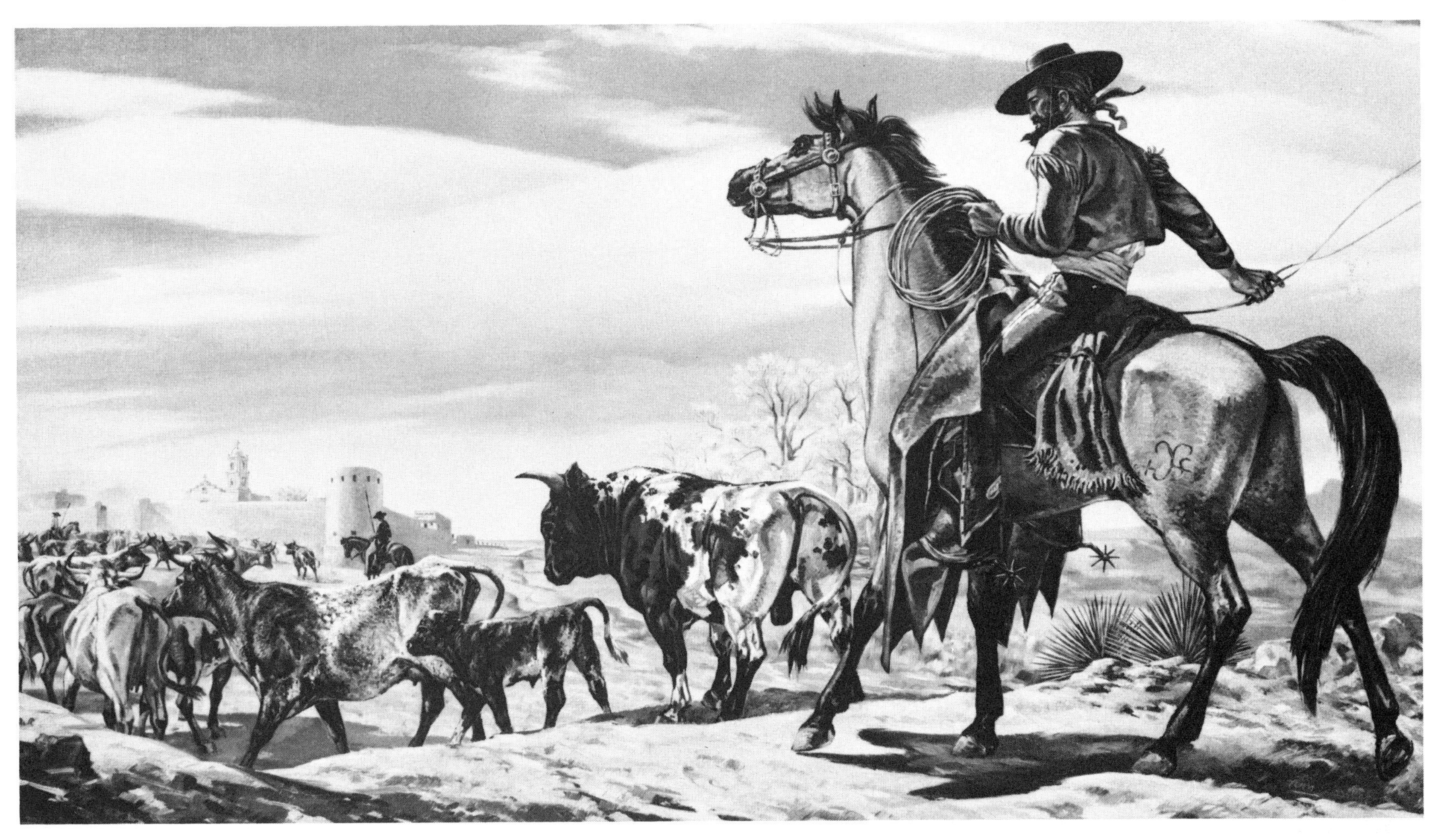

CATTLE ON AN EARLY MEXICAN HACIENDA, Tom Lea, oil, 20"x34"
Lent by Dallas Museum of Fine Arts, Dallas, Texas

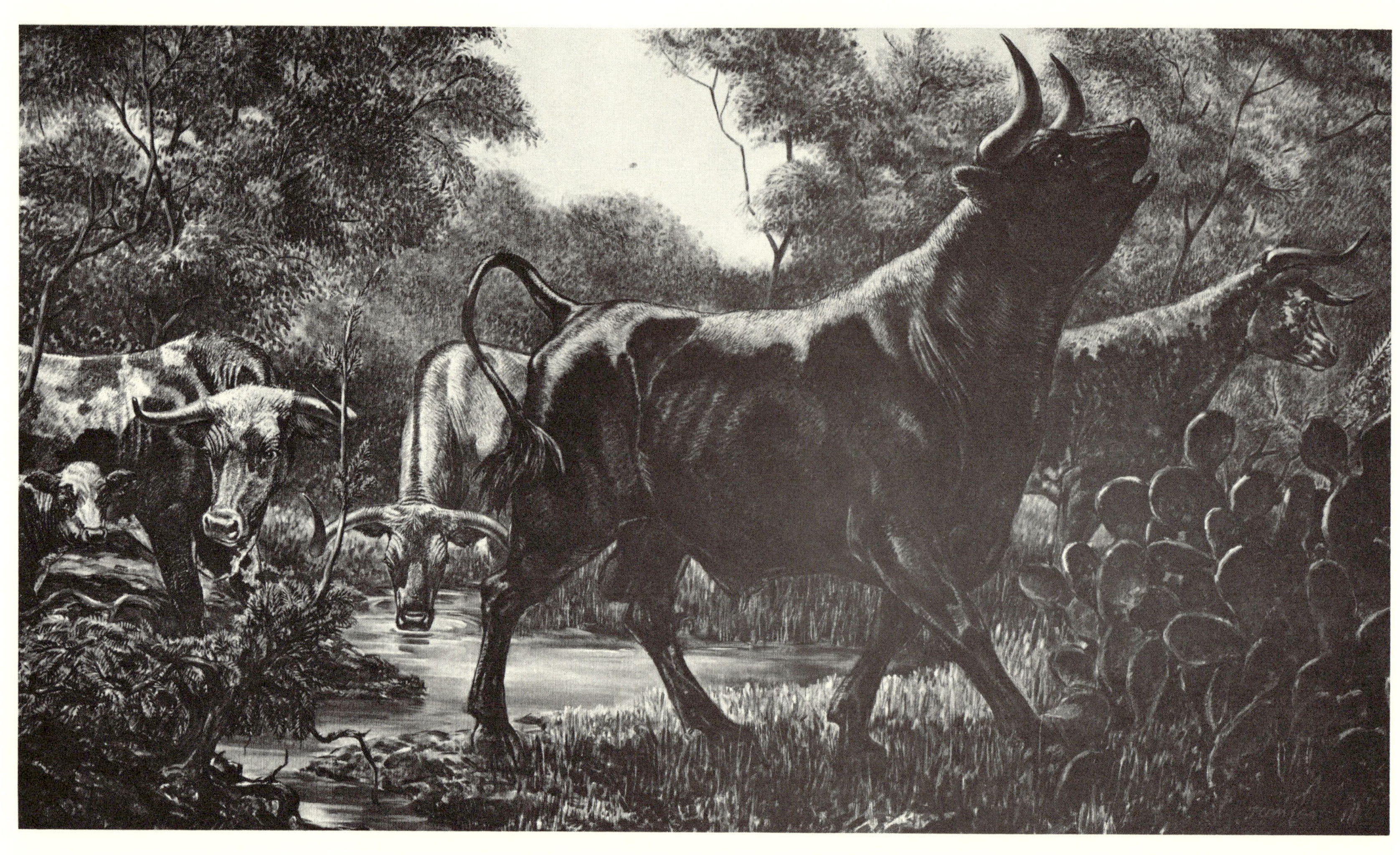

WILD CATTLE OF SOUTH TEXAS: ANCESTORS OF THE LONGHORNS, Tom Lea, oil, 20"x34"
Lent by Dallas Museum of Fine Arts, Dallas, Texas

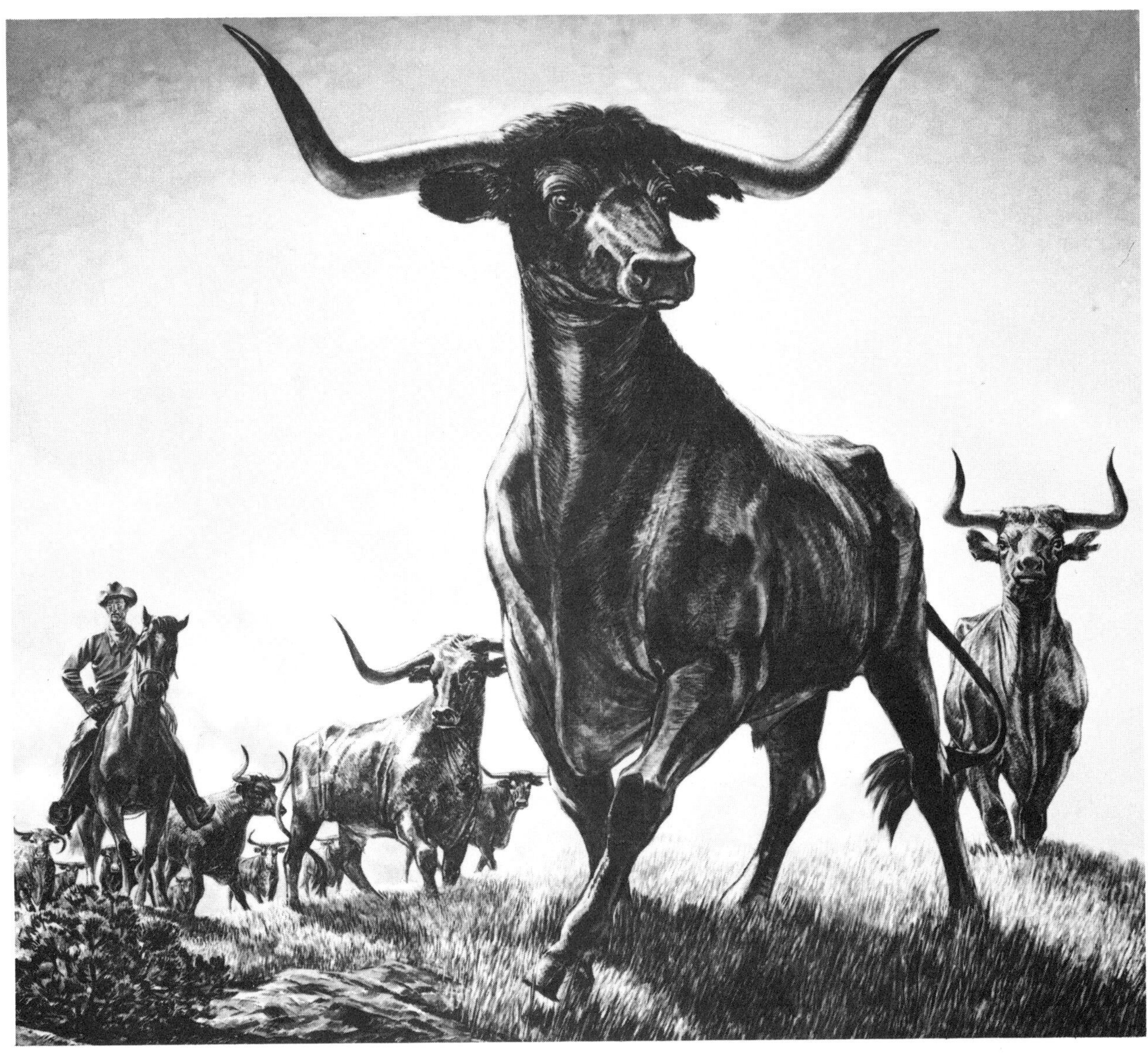

TEXAS LONGHORNS, Tom Lea, oil, 32"x34"
Lent by Dallas Museum of Fine Arts, Dallas, Texas

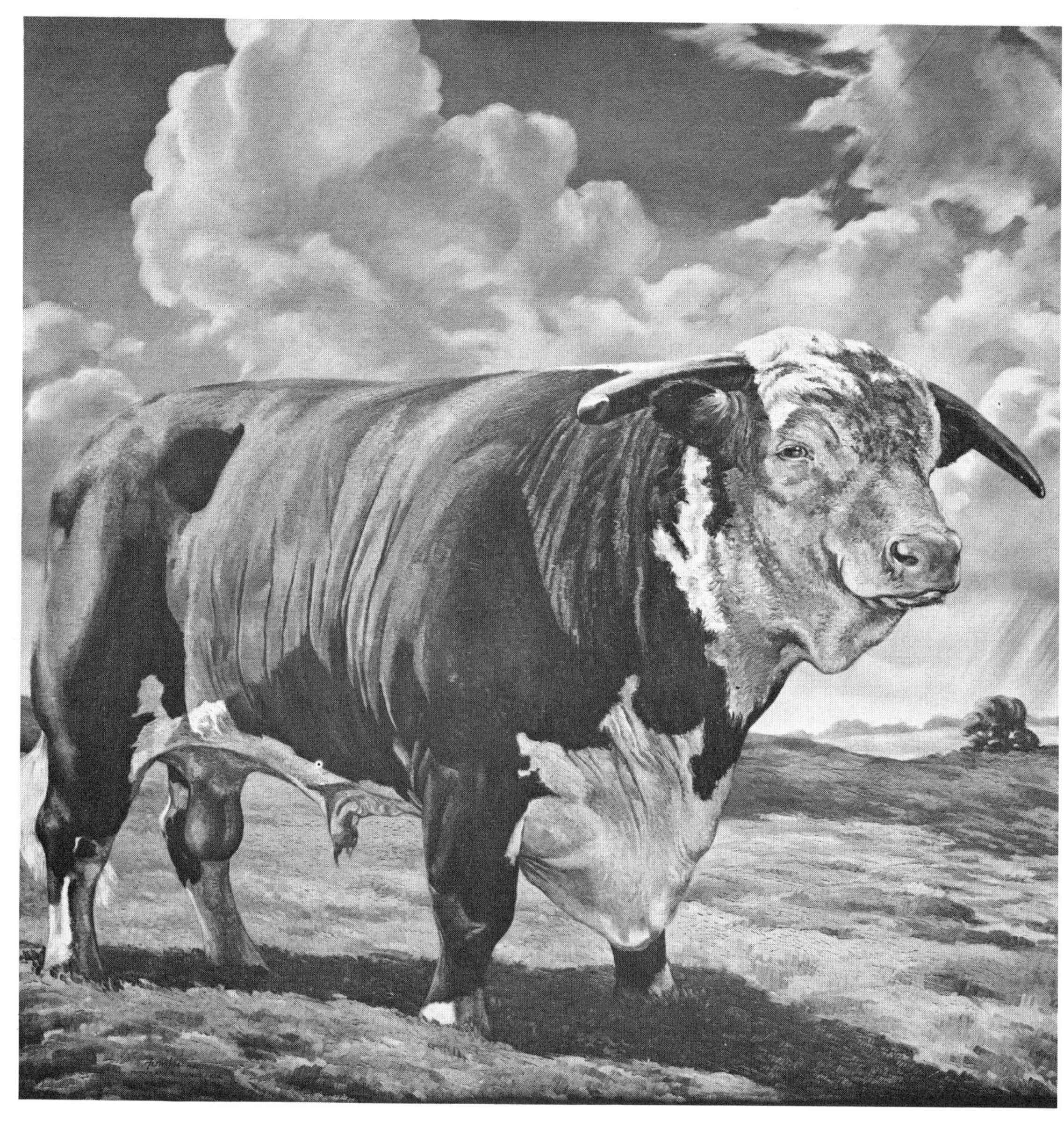

PORTRAIT OF HAZFORD RUPERT 81st, Tom Lea, oil, 34"x32"
Lent by Dallas Museum of Fine Arts, Dallas, Texas

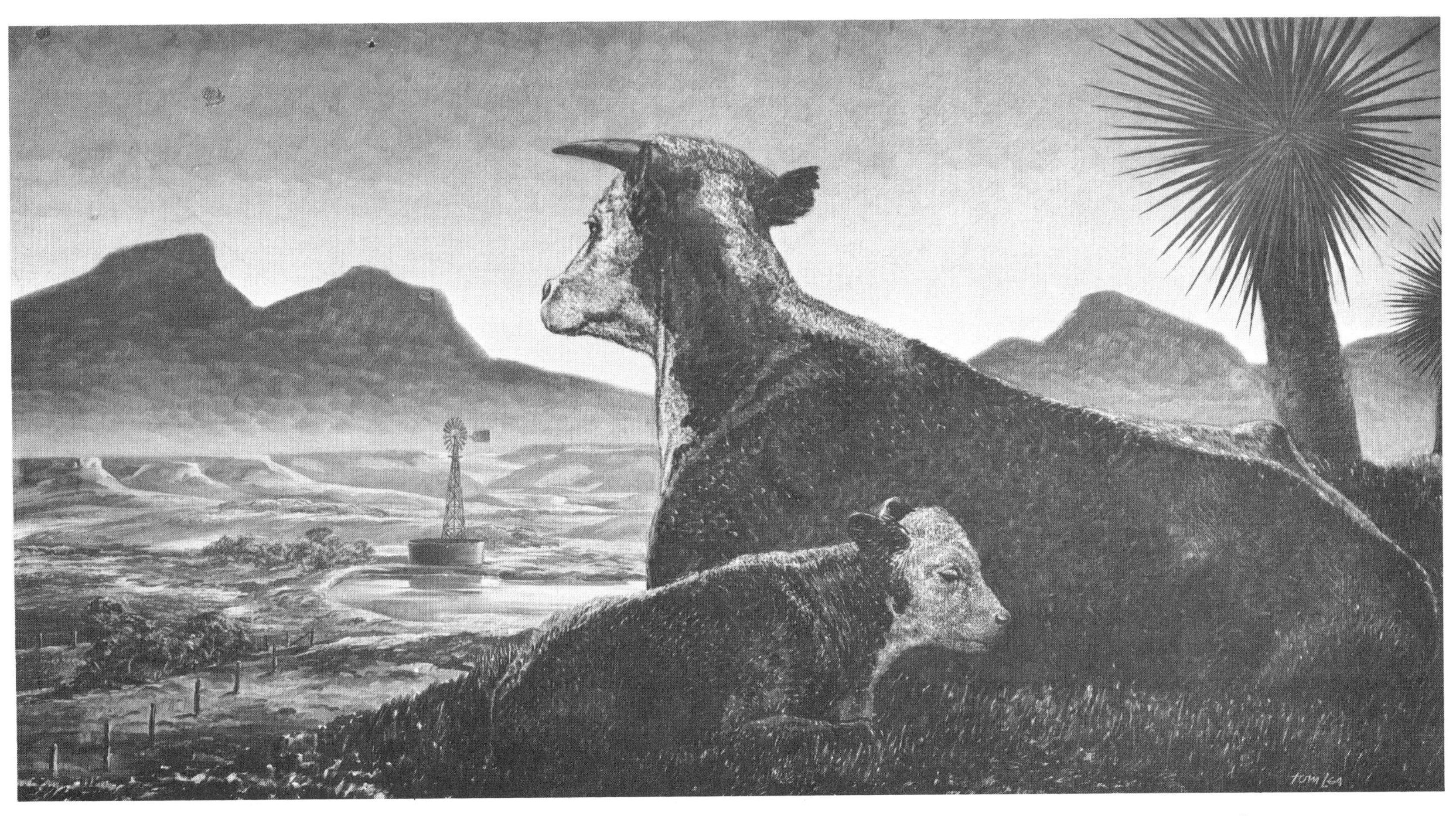

RANGE COW AND BEEF CALF, Tom Lea, oil, 18"x32"
Lent by Dallas Museum of Fine Arts, Dallas, Texas

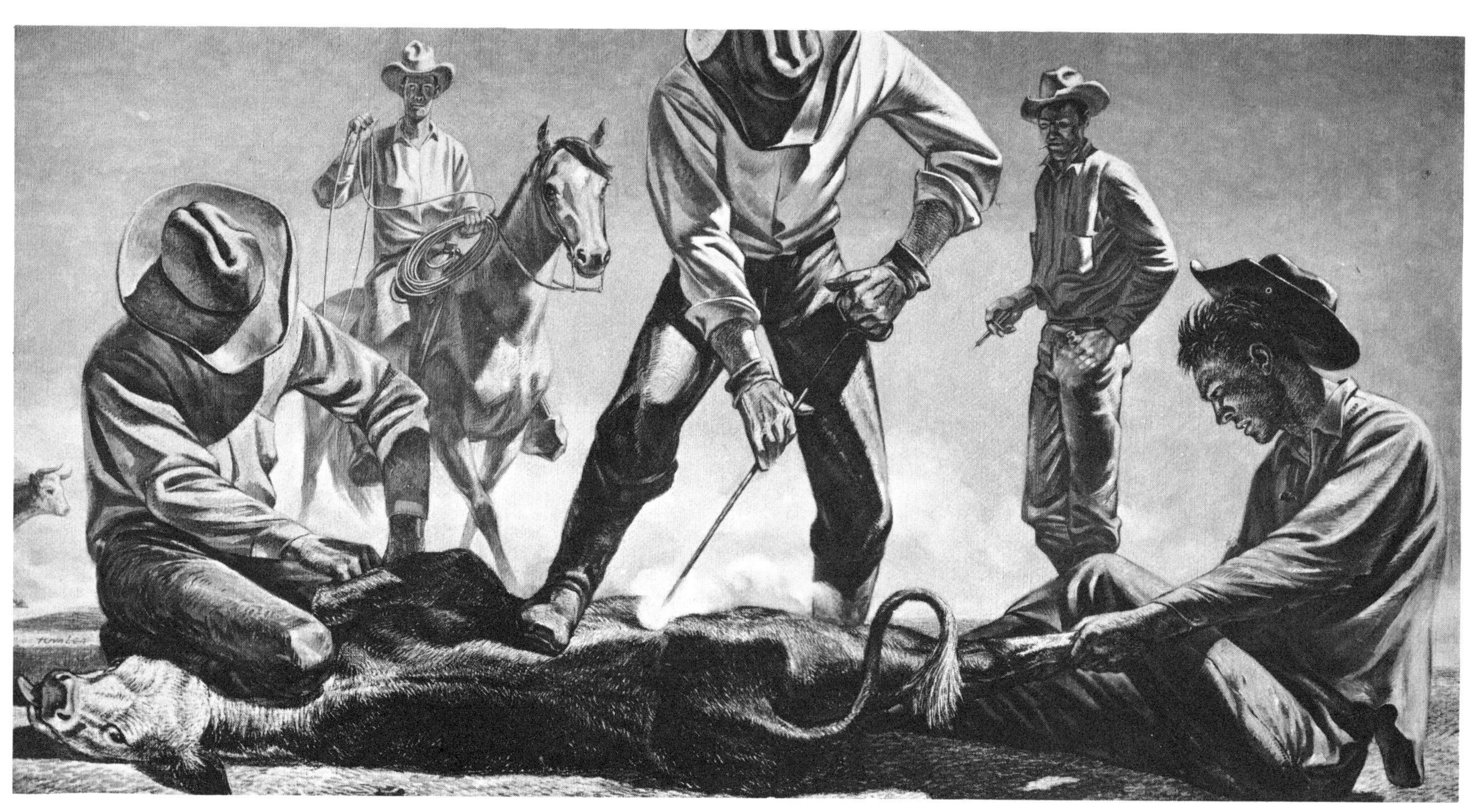

ROUND UP TIME: BRANDING A CALF, Tom Lea, oil, 18"x32"
Lent by Dallas Museum of Fine Arts, Dallas, Texas

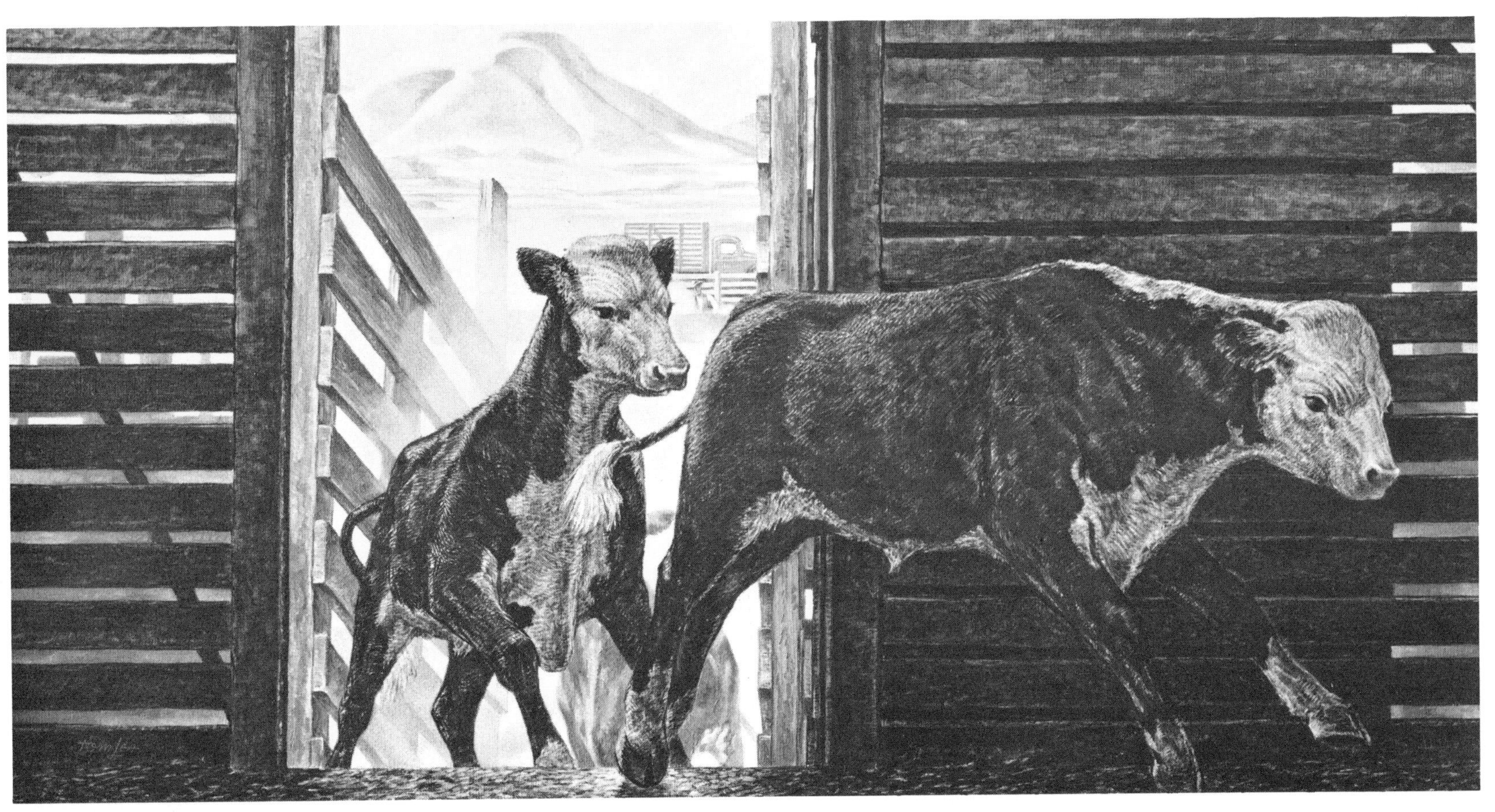

MOVING YOUNG BEEF STEERS FROM THE RANGE, Tom Lea, oil, 18"x32"
Lent by Dallas Museum of Fine Arts, Dallas, Texas

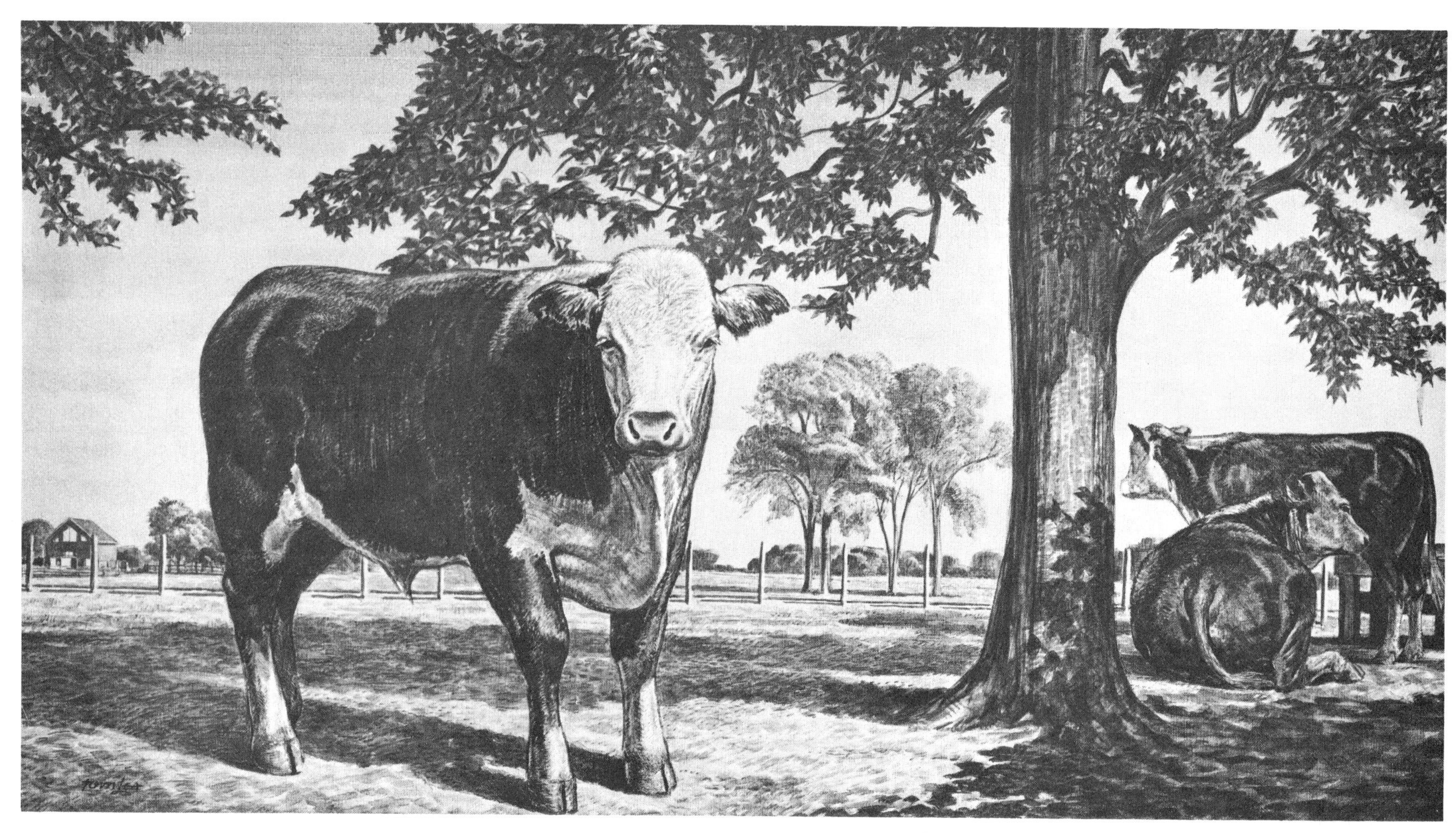

BEEF STEERS IN FEED LOT, Tom Lea, oil, 18"x32"
Lent by Dallas Museum of Fine Arts, Dallas, Texas

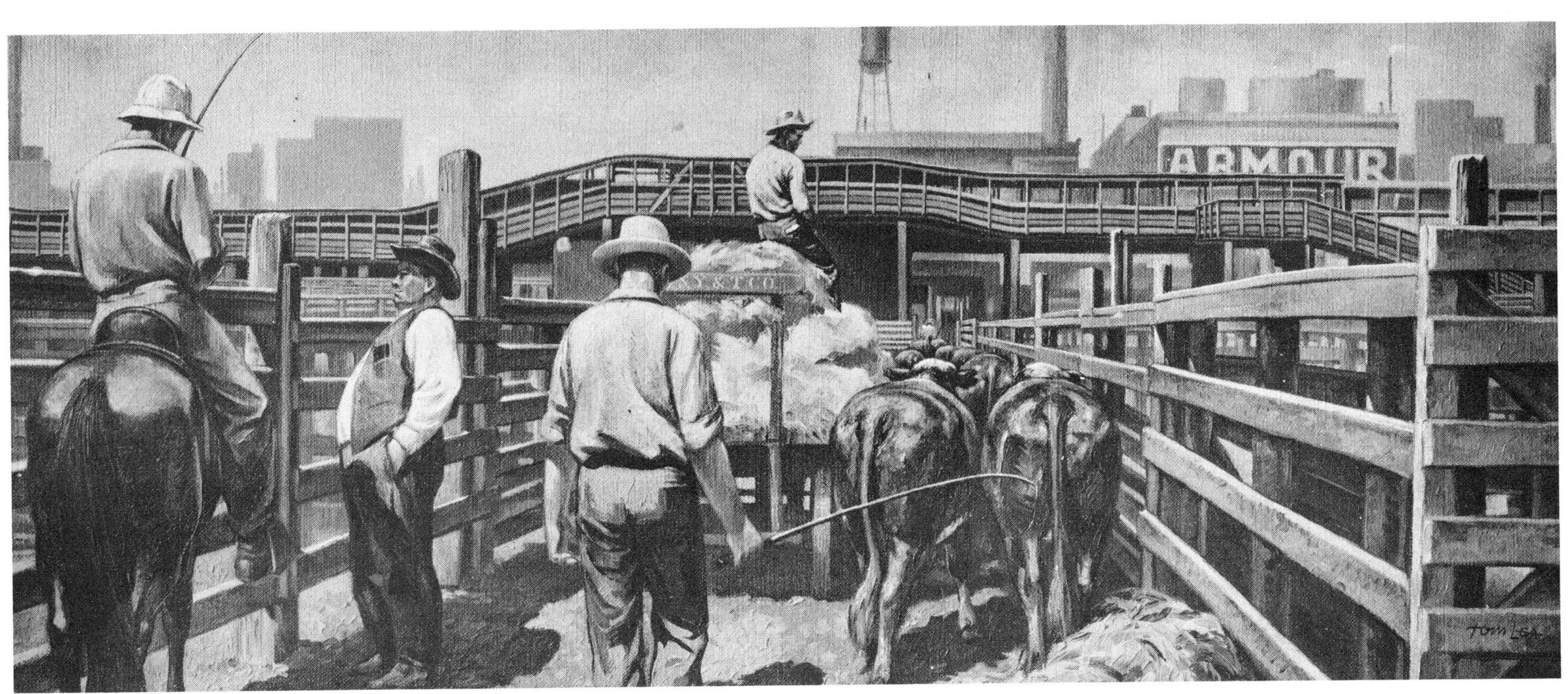

MOVING TO SLAUGHTER, UNION STOCKYARDS, CHICAGO, Tom Lea, oil, 12"x28"
Lent by Dallas Museum of Fine Arts, Dallas, Texas

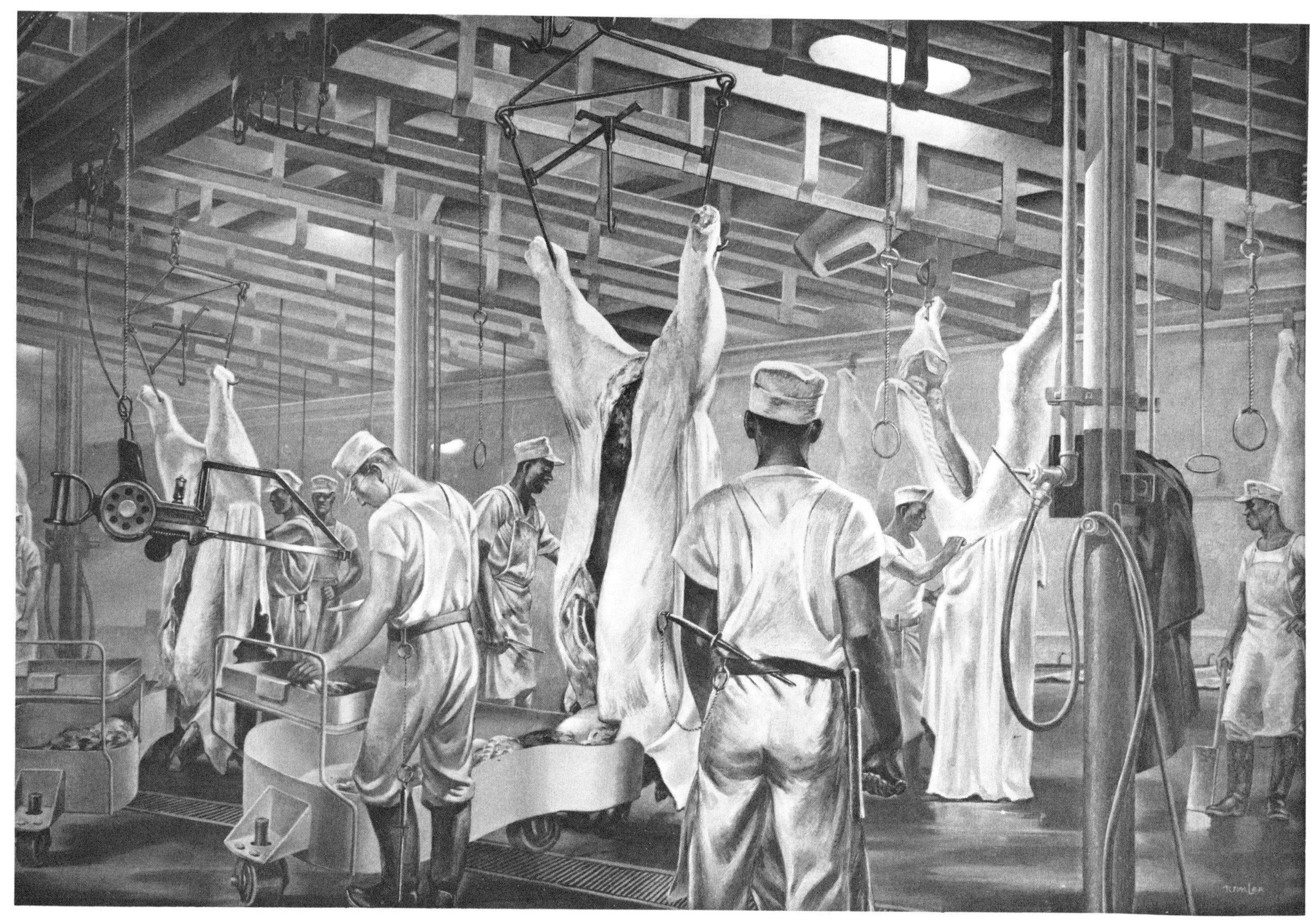

DRESSING BEEF: SWIFT & CO., CHICAGO, Tom Lea, oil, 22"x32"
Lent by Dallas Museum of Fine Arts, Dallas, Texas

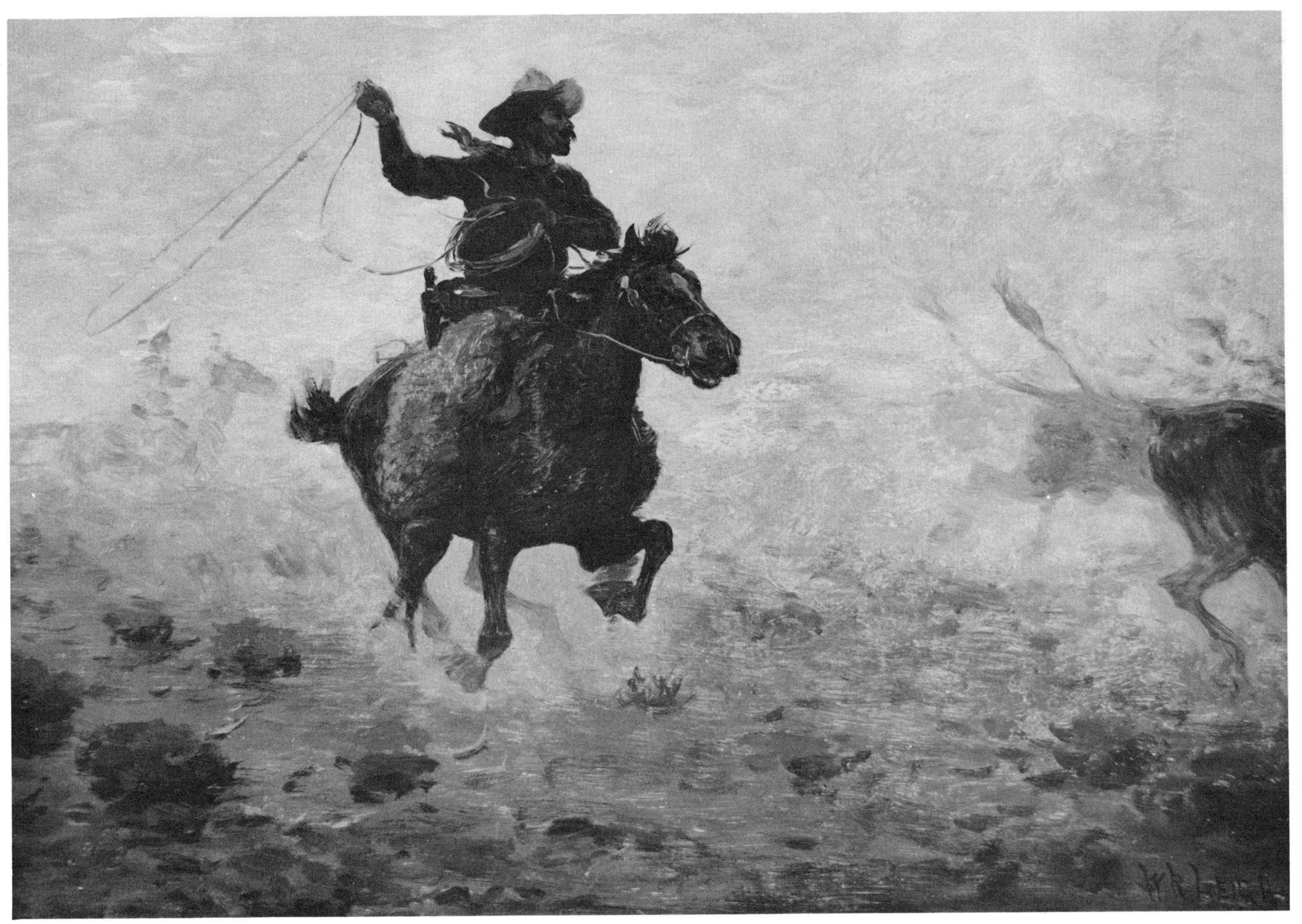

RIDING COWBOY, W. R. Leigh, oil, 12"x16"
Lent by William J. Williams Family

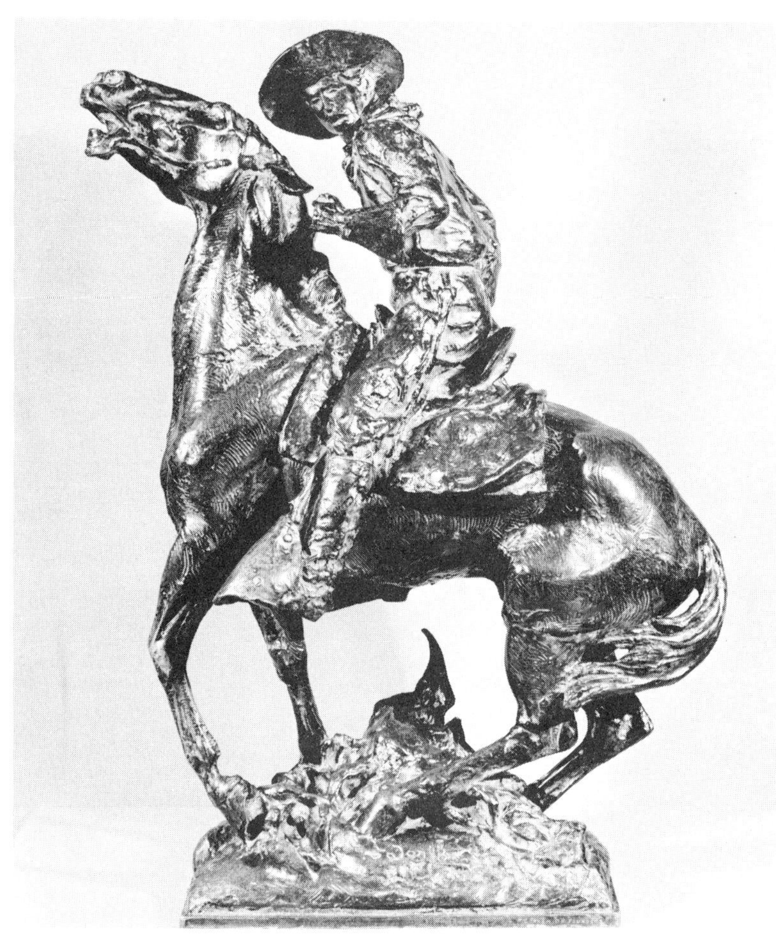

BUCKY O'NEIL, Solon Borglum, bronze
Permanent Collection of the Whitney Gallery of Western Art

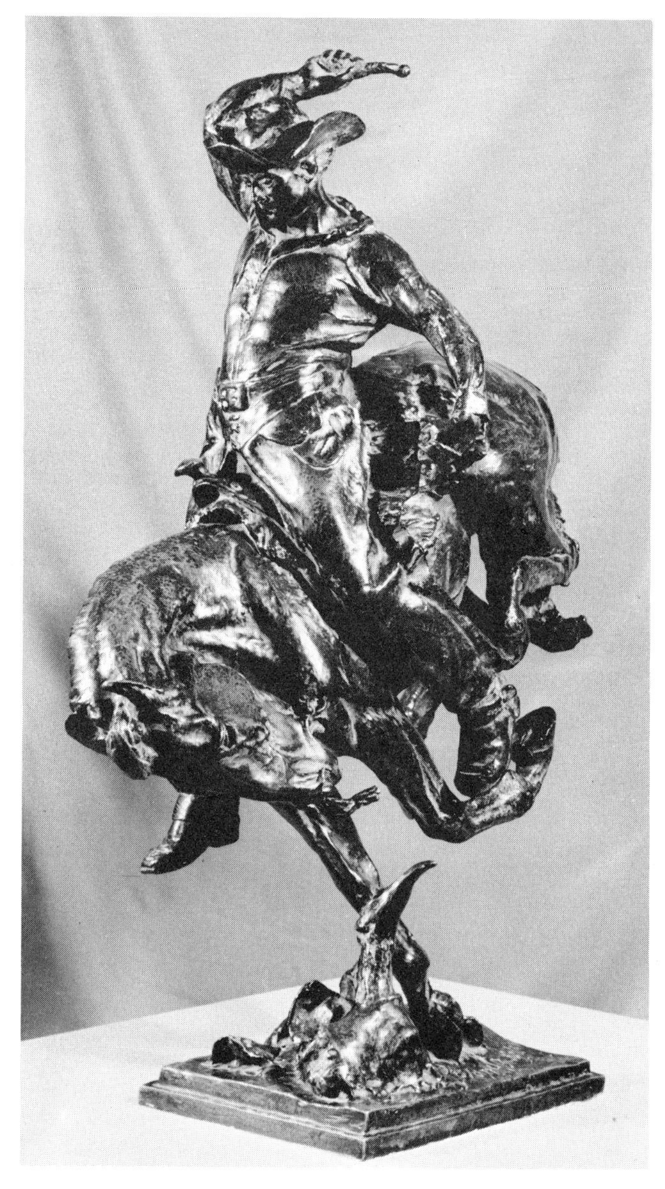

BRONCO BUSTER, Solon Borglum, bronze
Permanent collection of the Whitney Gallery of Western Art

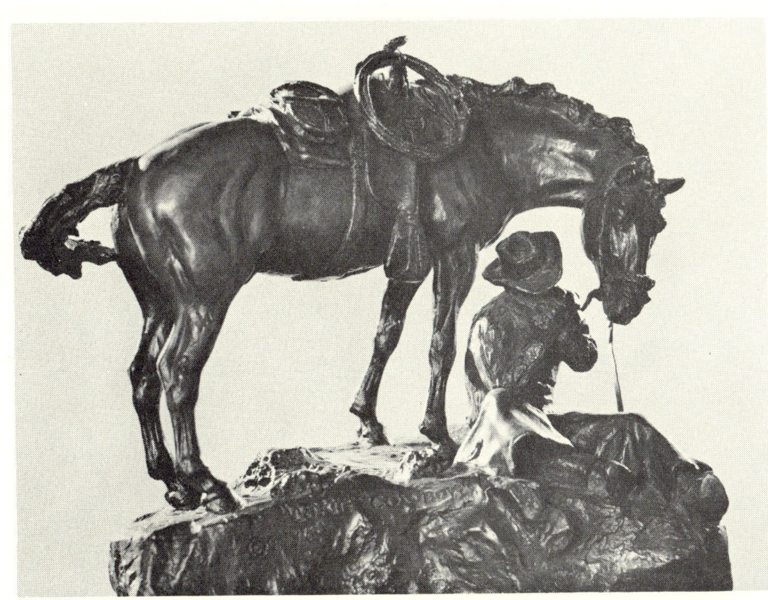

LONE COWBOY, Bob Scriver, bronze
Lent by the artist

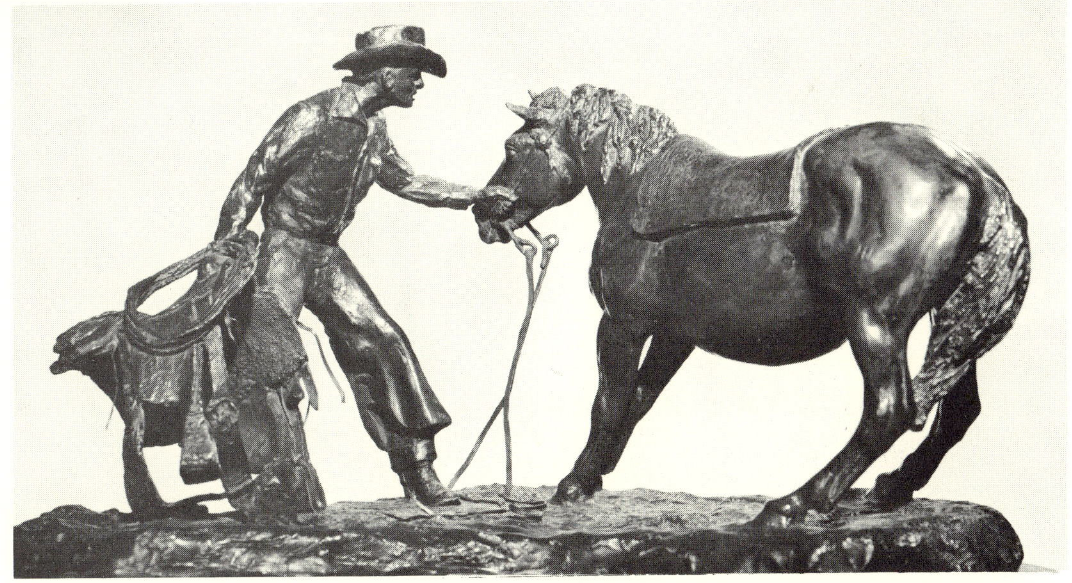

4 O'CLOCK IN THE MORNING, Bob Scriver, bronze
Lent by the artist

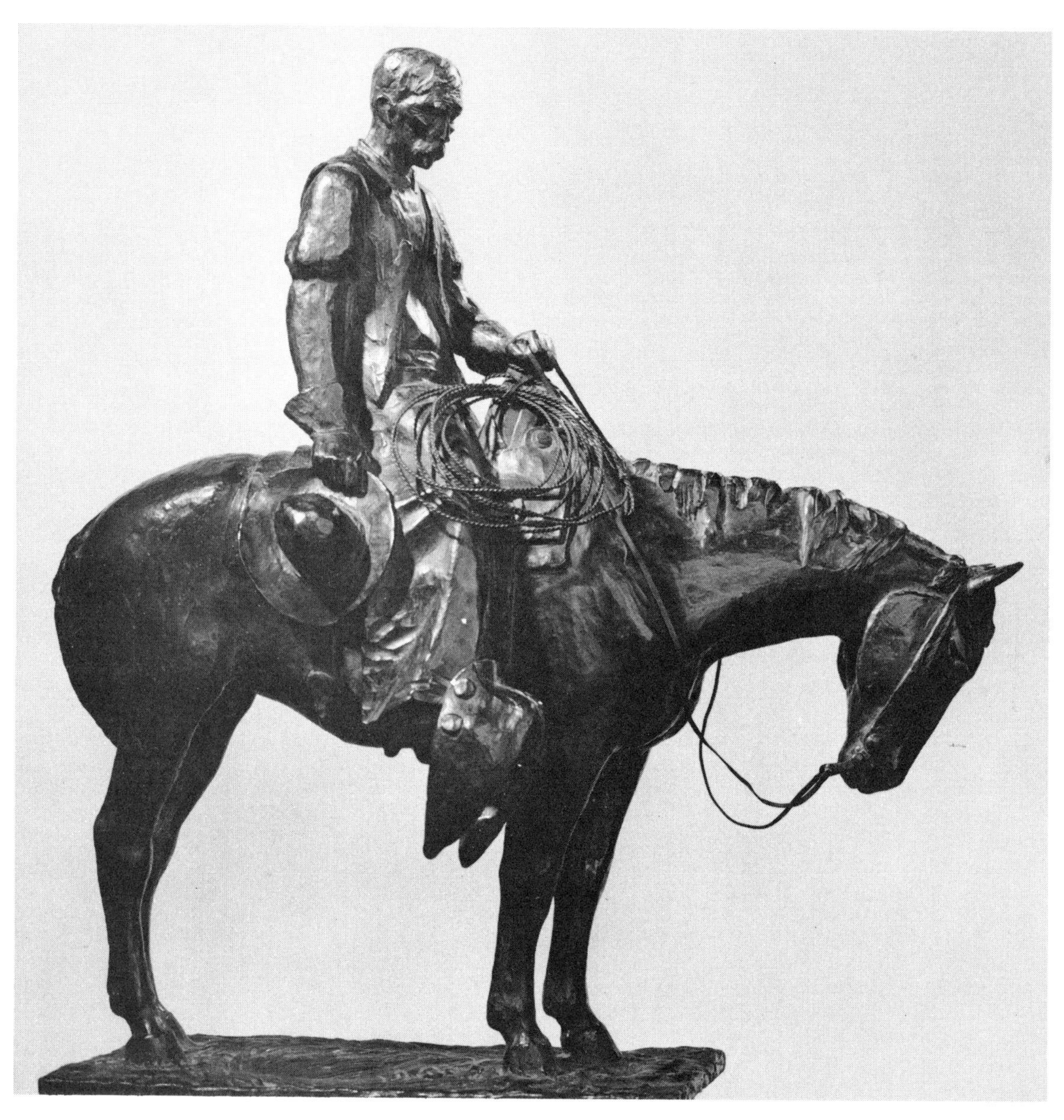

COWBOY MEDITATION, Harry Jackson, bronze
Permanent collection of the Whitney Gallery of Western Art

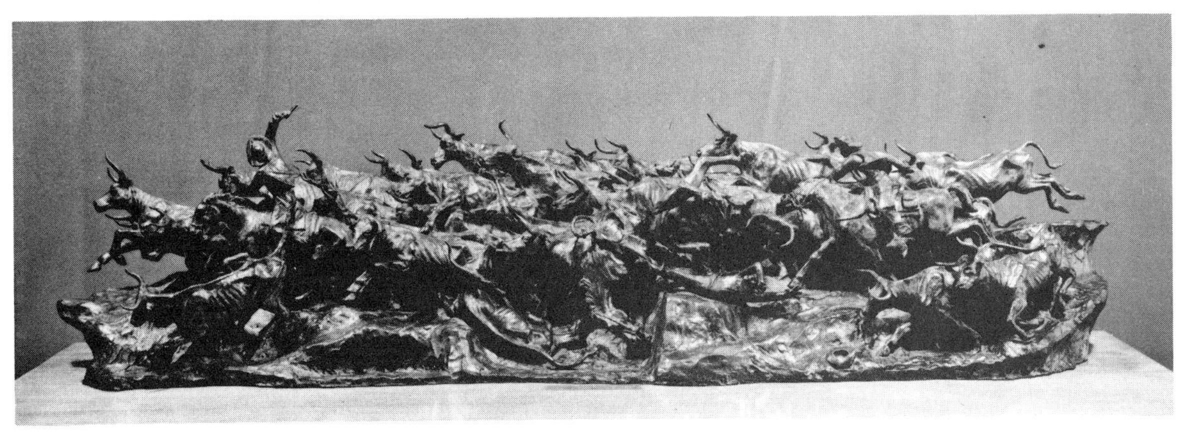

STAMPEDE, Harry Jackson, bronze
Permanent collection of the Whitney Gallery of Western Art

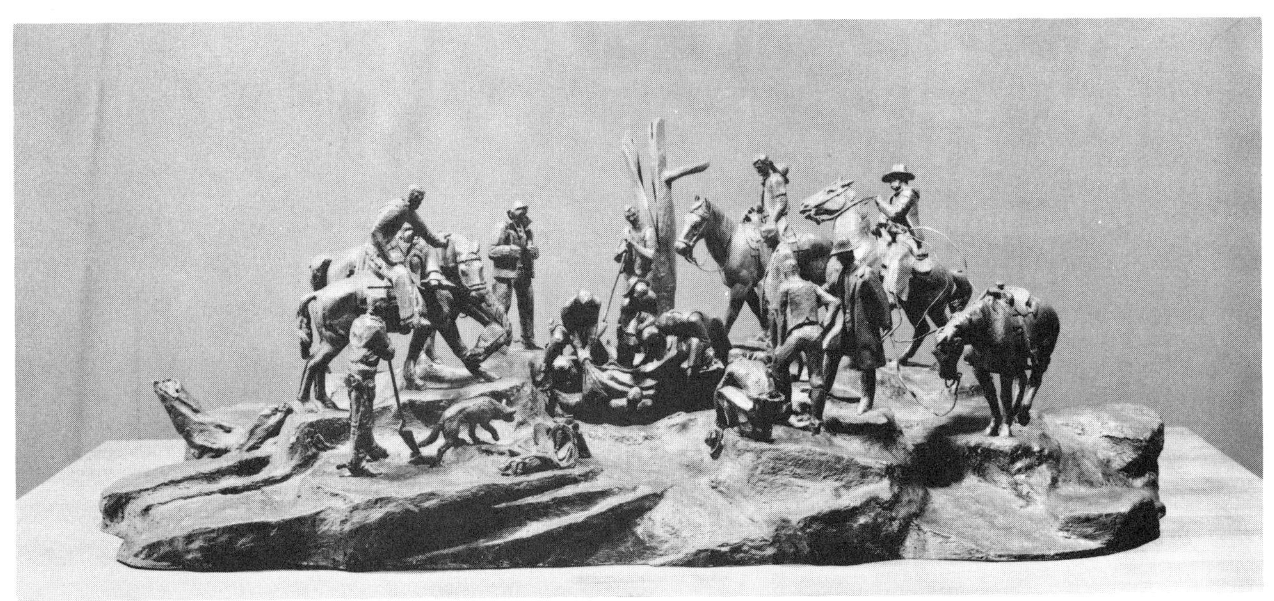

THE COWBOY BURIAL, Harry Jackson, bronze
Permanent collection of the Whitney Gallery of Western Art

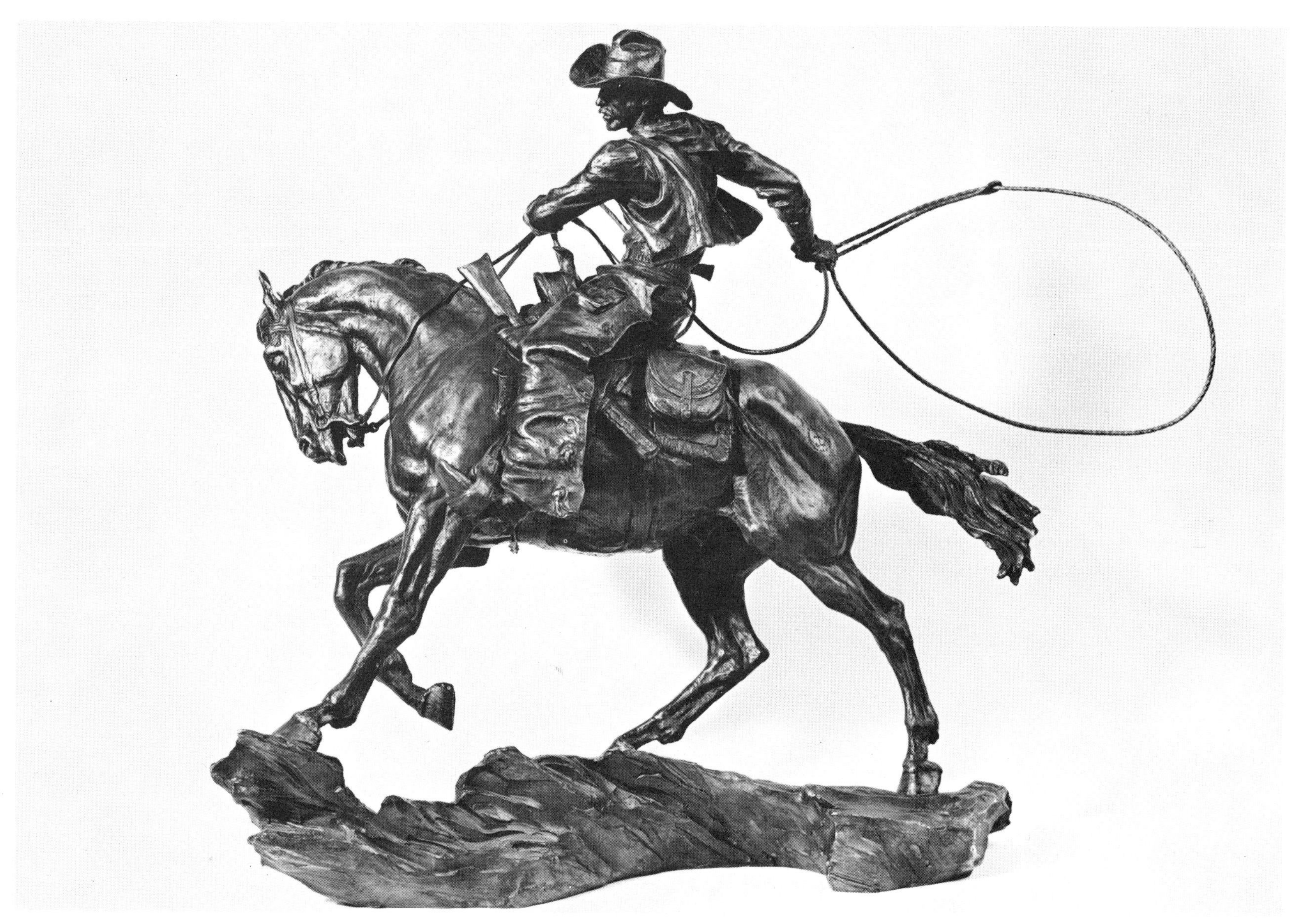

THE GREAT AMERICAN COWBOY, Edward J. Fraughton, bronze
Lent by the artist

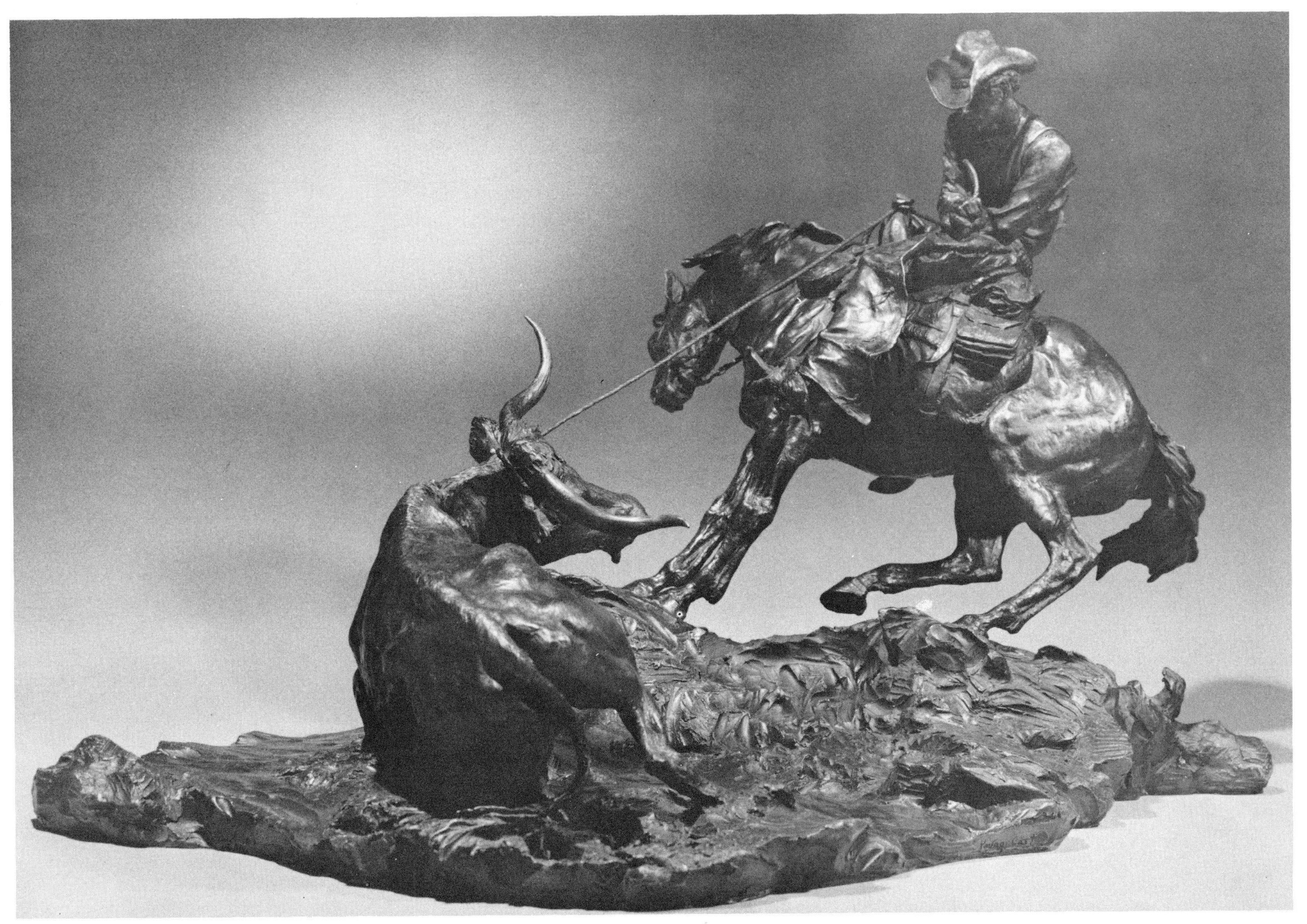

BOG RIDER, Edward J. Fraughton, bronze
Lent by the artist

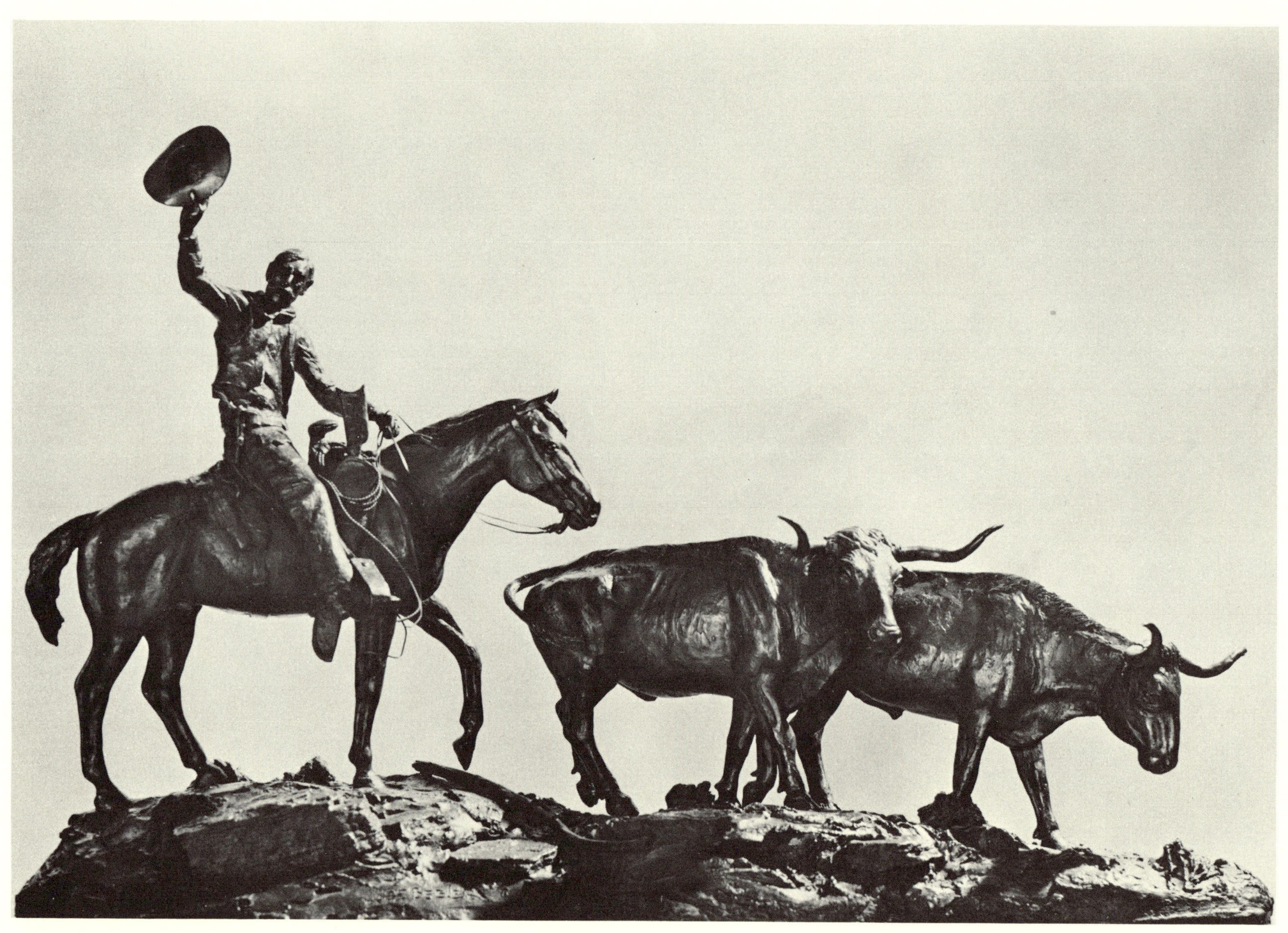

UP THE TRAIL, Joe Beeler, bronze
Lent by the artist

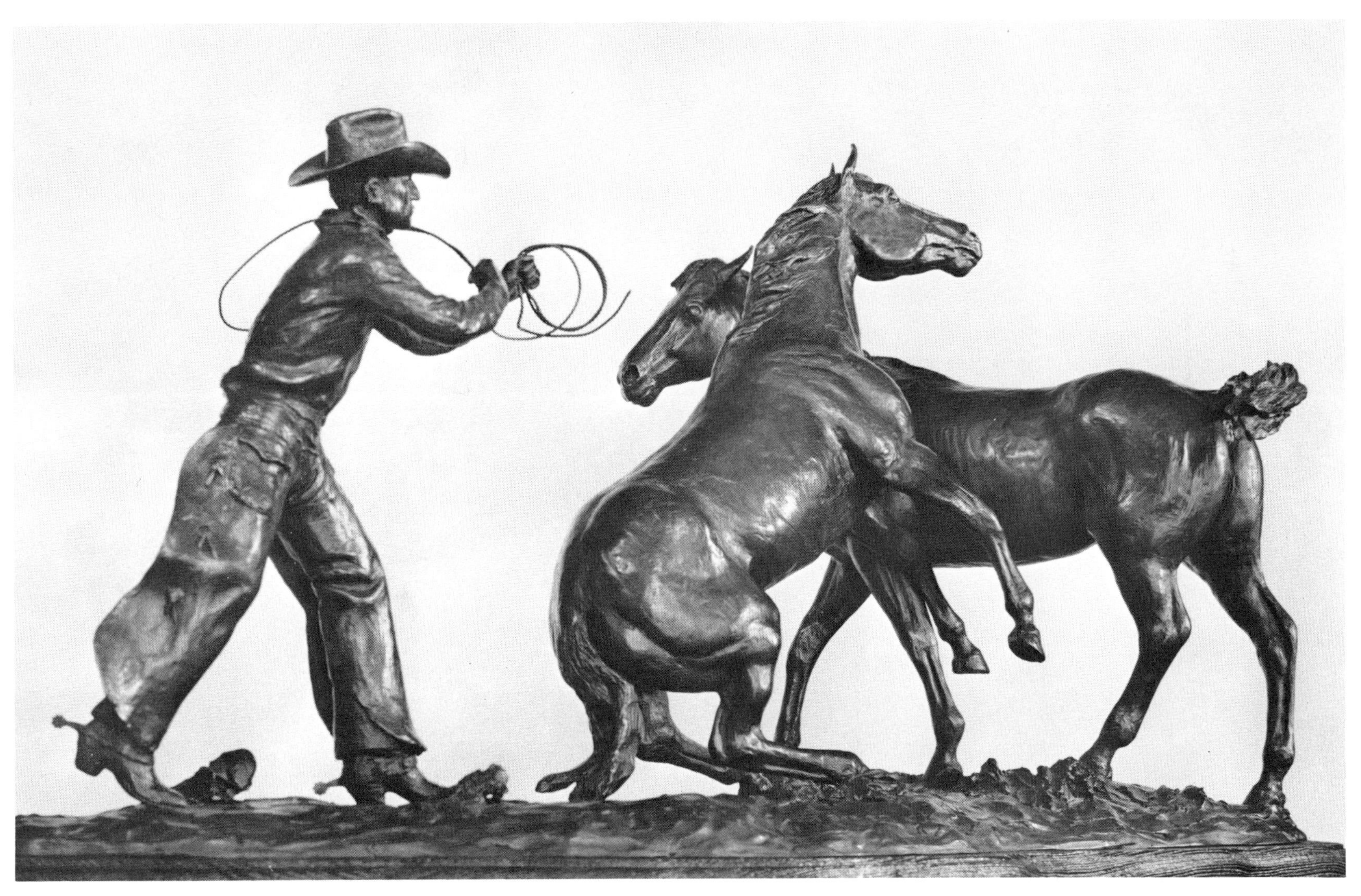

STARTING THE DAY, Joe Beeler, bronze
Lent by the artist

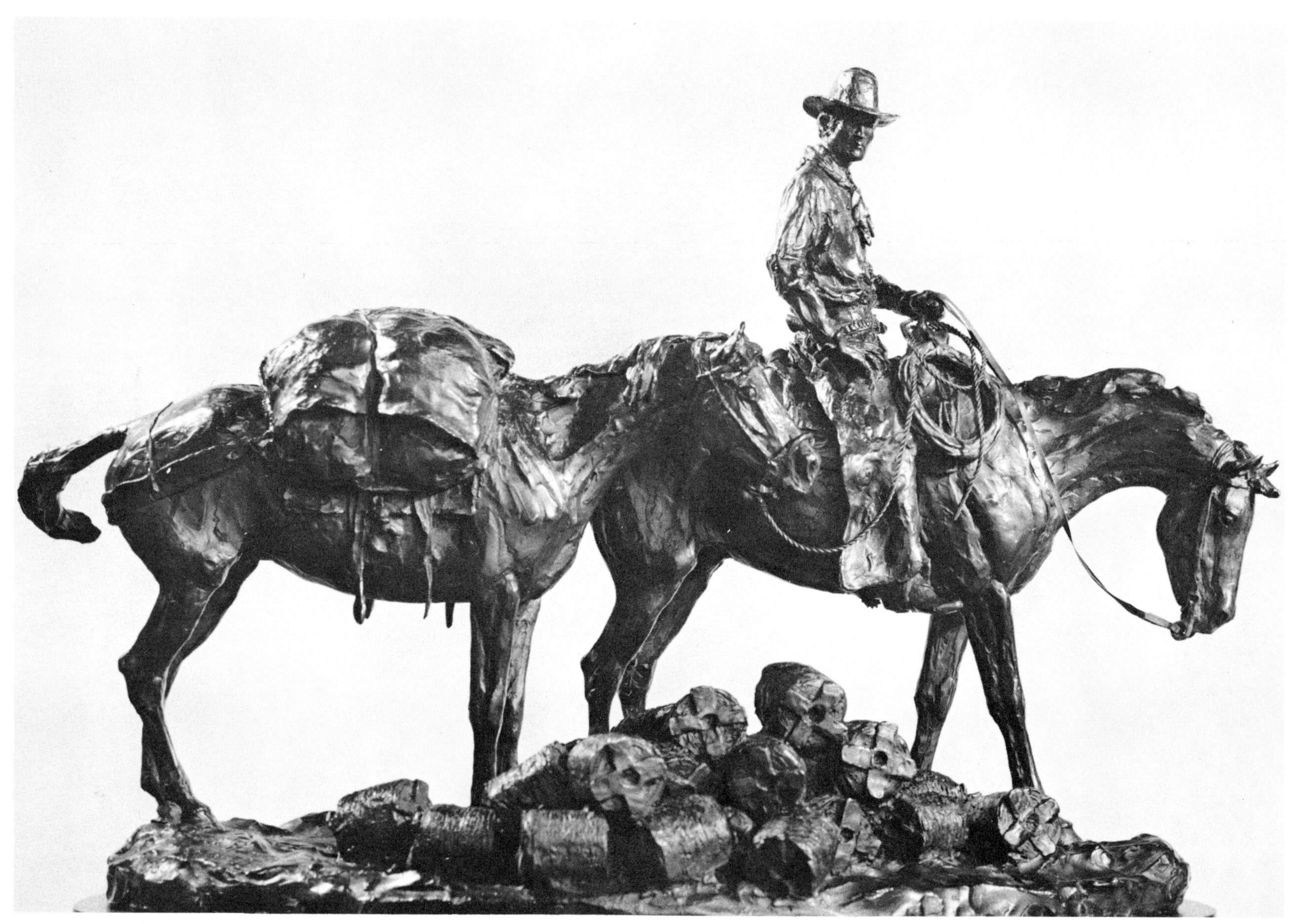

END OF THE OPEN RANGE, Grant Speed, bronze
Lent by the artist

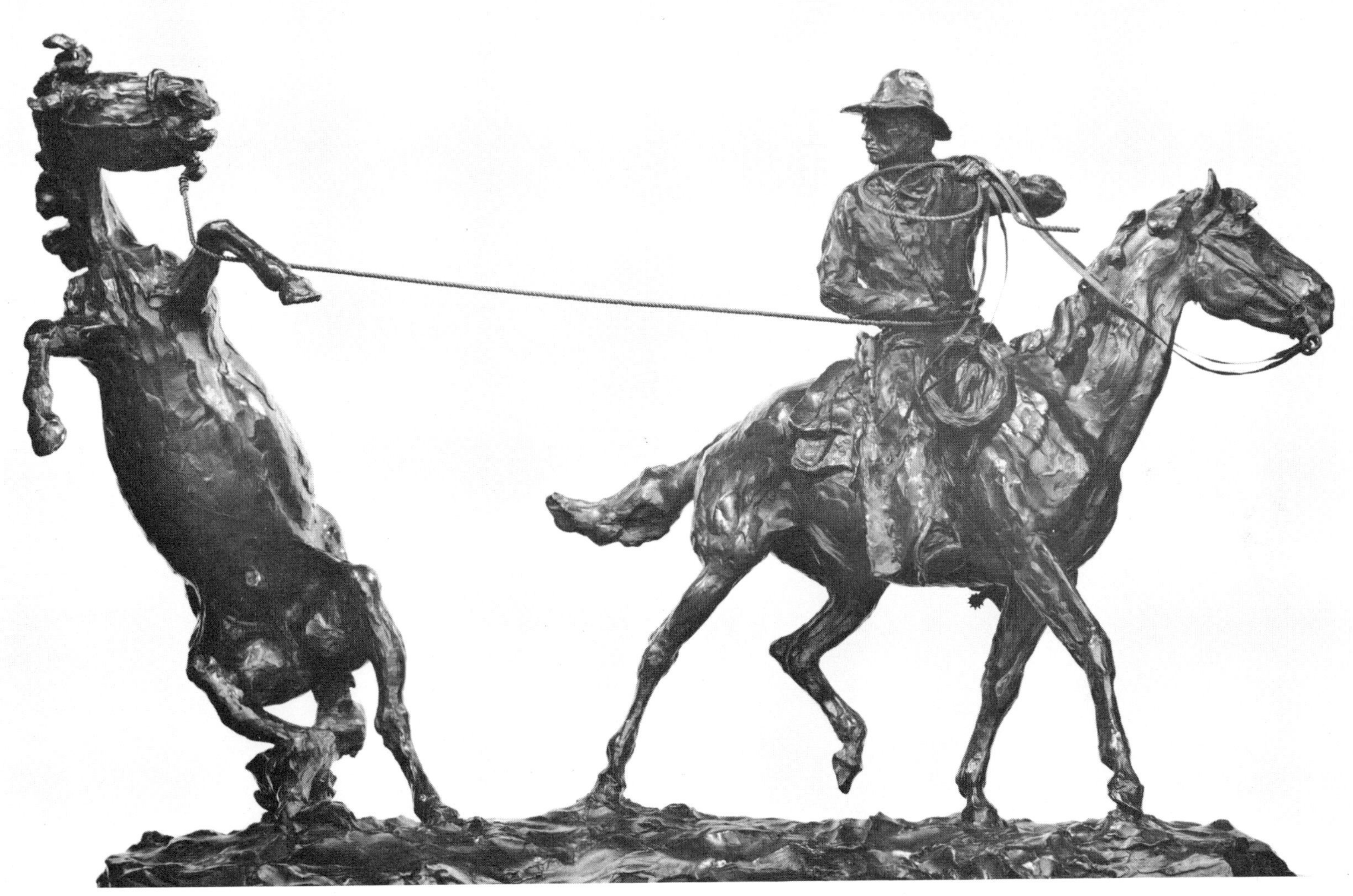

FIRST FEEL OF THE HACKAMORE, Grant Speed, bronze
Lent by the artist

NICK EGGENHOFER

Nick Eggenhofer (born 1897) is one of the most prolific of all the artists who have used Western subject matter. He has produced about thirty thousand sketches, drawings, and paintings. The majority of his efforts have appeared as illustrations in magazines and books.

Eggenhofer was born in Southern Bavaria and came to the United States when he was sixteen. While working as an apprentice at the American Lithograph Company in New York, he attended night classes in art at Cooper Union. His interest in the West goes back to his German boyhood, when William F. Cody's Wild West Show had made a highly successful continental tour. Eggenhofer's initial art effort had Western subjects, although he had not yet visited the West.

The aspiring artist found a large market for his drawings in the Western pulps of the publishing house of Street and Smith. During the following decades, Eggenhofer visited the West often and continually added to his extensive research files. His signature became well known to the readers of Western stories.

Since moving to Cody, Wyoming, in 1961, Eggenhofer has concentrated on painting. His most effective efforts have been in the medium of gouache, essentially watercolor prepared with gum binder to give the paint a body and opacity which approaches the quality of oil. Eggenhofer is widely recognized for his accurate depiction of early Western horse-drawn transportation. In 1961 his definitive work on this subject, WAGONS, MULES AND MEN, was published. He has also executed several sculptures which have been cast in bronze in recent years.

Eggenhofer does not shun the label of illustrator. In this regard he says: "I have always liked to paint pictures that tell a story. There is plenty of room for imagination and creativity. The problems presented in doing a good illustration can be just as challenging artistically as in a painting to hang on a wall."

We are pleased to include an exhibition of Nick Eggenhofer's art for our 1975 season at the Buffalo Bill Historical Center. Special thanks are due to a number of persons who lent pieces from their private collections. These friends of ours, and of Nick's, include: J. O. Keeley, Jess and Polly Frost, Dick Frost, Mac Taggart, all of Cody; Paul and Doris Masa of Kalispell, Montana, Bob Rockwell of Corning, New York, L. W. Taggart of Las Vegas, Nevada; and a large number of pieces from the personal collection of Nick and Louisa Eggenhofer.

Dick Frost, Curator of the Buffalo Bill Museum arranged the exhibition and we appreciate Nick's enthusiastic assistance.

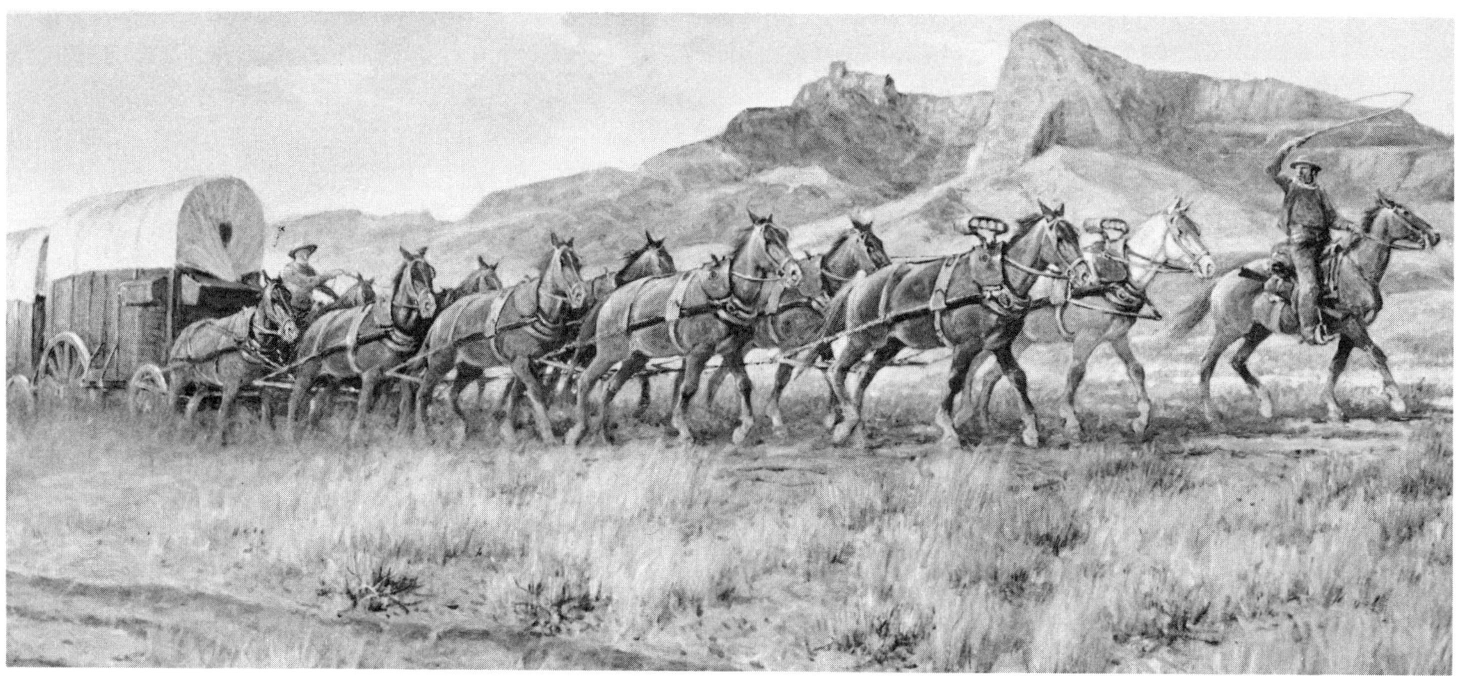

WYOMING STRING TEAM, Nick Eggenhofer, oil, 28"x58"
Permanent collection of the Whitney Gallery of Western Art

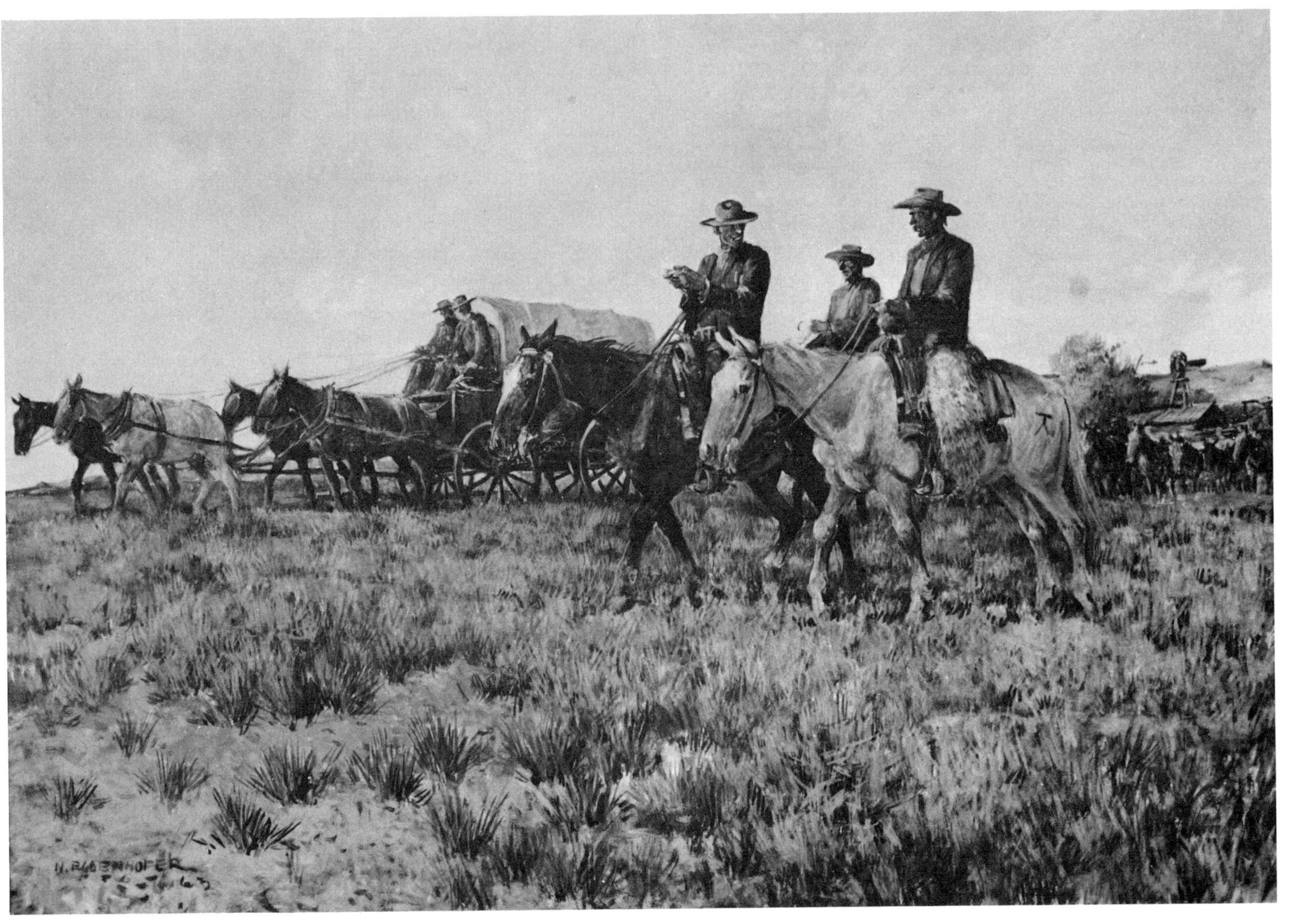

ROUNDUP MORNING, Nick Eggenhofer, gouache, 9"x13"
Lent by the Rockwell Foundation, Corning, New York

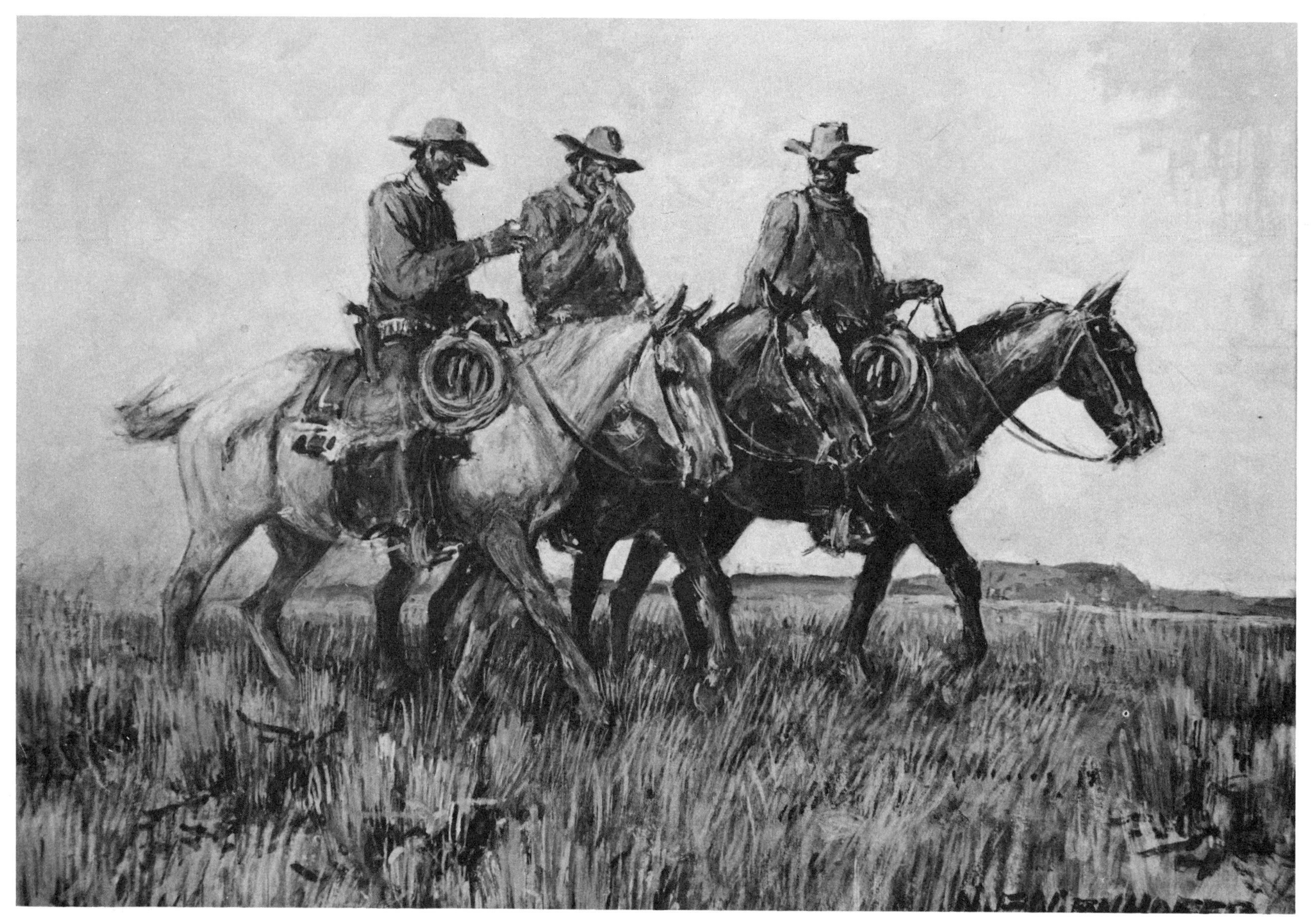

COWBOYS THREE, Nick Eggenhofer, gouache, 8"x10¼"
Lent by Dick Frost

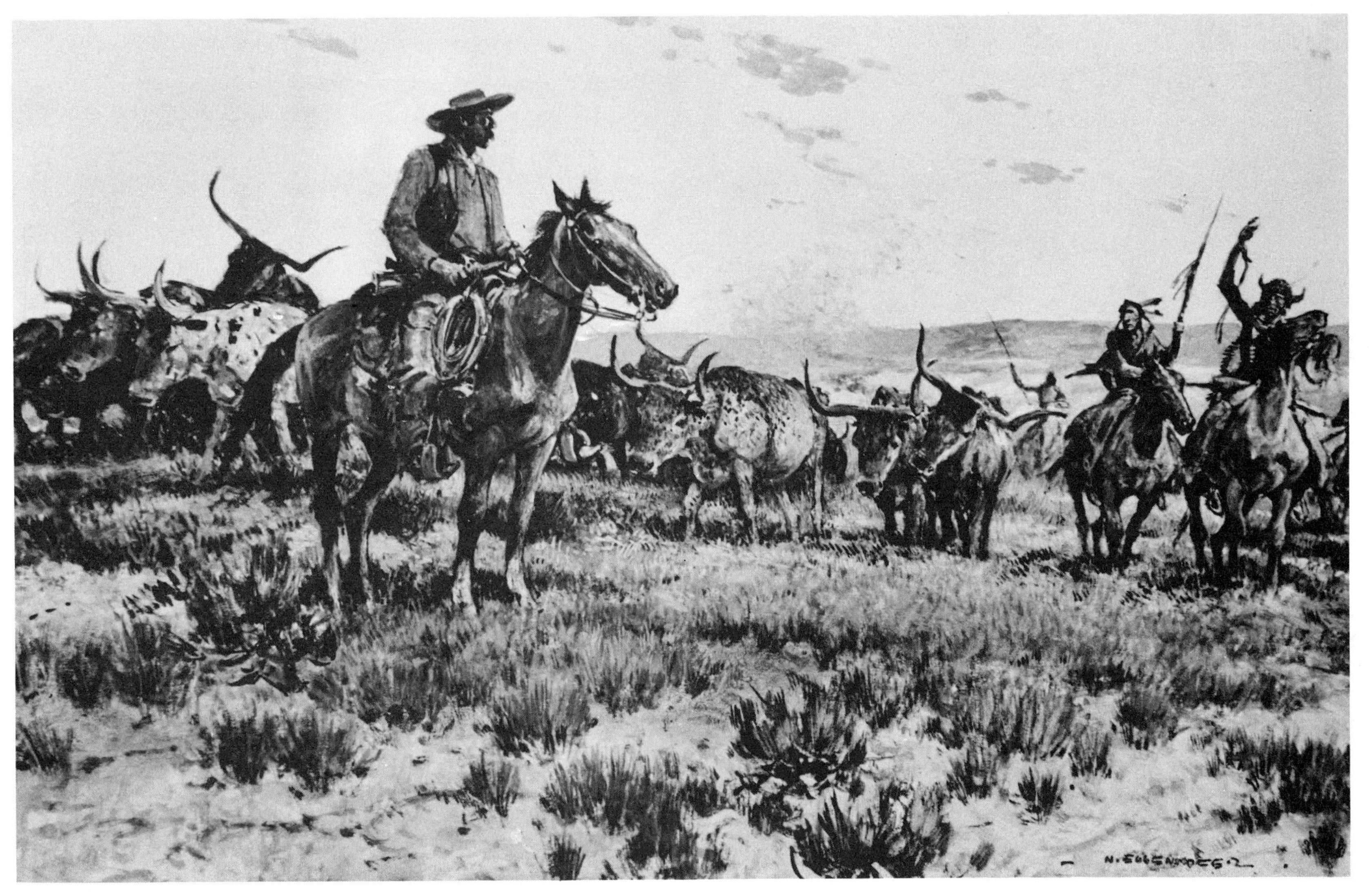

DAKOTA COUNTRY, Nick Eggenhofer, gouache, 21"x30"
Lent by the Rockwell Foundation, Corning, New York

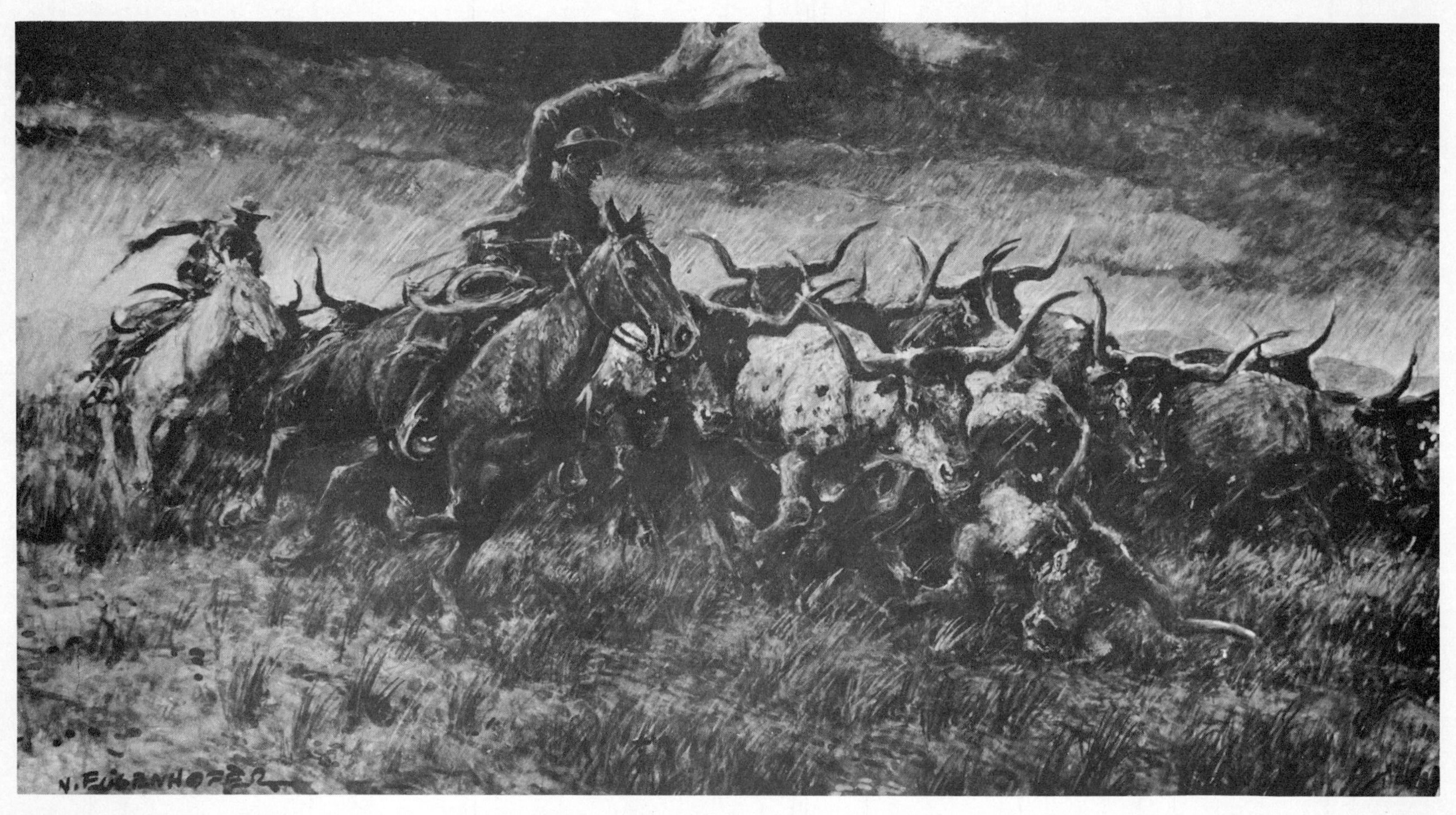

THE STAMPEDE, Nick Eggenhofer, gouache, 16"x28"
Lent from the Eggenhofer collection